y Memory:
We Forget Some Things and Remember Others

By

Robert Guarino

Illustrations by

Jeff Jackson

Hoopoe Books

HOOPOE

Published by Hoopoe Books
a division of The Institute for the Study of Human Knowledge

Copyright © 2009 by The Institute for the Study of Human Knowledge
Illustrations copyright © 2009 by Jeff Jackson

Foreword by Robert Ornstein, Ph.D.

General Editors: Denise Nessel, Ph.D., and Robert Ornstein, Ph.D.

Content Standards Alignment by Brett Wiley, M.A. Education

ISBN 978-1-933779-64-5

Me and My Memory:
Why We Forget Some Things and Remember Others

Contents

Foreword
Open During Remodeling

Now that's a sign you don't see very often, and for good reason. Ask anyone who has had to live in a home while remodeling was going on in the kitchen or bathroom. Most businesses just close up shop while the place is being torn up and put back together. Remodels are messy, disruptive and downright inconvenient. But that's exactly what's going on in your brain!

There was once a time when all the changes that occurred around puberty were blamed on hormones. Now, we're not letting the surge in chemicals through your body off the hook, but today scientific research reveals that a second growth spurt in the brain also contributes to the changes that occur during the teenage years. Surprisingly, the changes to a teen's brain are similar to the growth of a baby's brain in the first eighteen months of life. A massive spurt of new brain cells called gray matter occurs, and nerve cells called neurons make new connections. Then slowly, throughout the teenage years and into the early twenties, cells that don't make connections are trimmed back.

Scientists speculate that this second growth spurt aids us all in adapting to the world. It seems this is the last chance in life to learn a new skill or develop a lifelong habit easily. If you take up a new skill or keep practicing at an old one, your brain will rewire itself to support these abilities at a faster rate than at any other time in your life. No wonder the teen years are such a good time to take up playing guitar or drum, or to learn Chinese or Italian! On the other hand, you want to avoid getting into some bad habits because these get wired in, too, and will be harder to change later on. Now is a really good time to learn some good habits for dealing with anger, stress, and self-control. Good habits learned now really could last a lifetime.

First, you should know that the frontal lobes are responsible for self-control, judgment, organization, planning, and emotional control. These are skills many teens struggle with in middle and high school as this part of the brain matures. And, according to research conducted by Giedd at the National Institute of Mental Health using Magnetic Resonance Imaging (MRI), a number of additional unexpected brain developments occur in people from ages 10 through mid-20s. This altered the previously held belief that a person's brain was fully mature by ages 8 to 10. MRIs first revealed that the corpus callosum, the part of the brain that connects the left and right hemispheres, continues to grow until a person is in their mid-20s.

While the implications of this are not fully known, the corpus callosum has been linked to intelligence and self-awareness. Elizabeth Sowell of UCLA's Lab of Neuro Imaging found that the frontal lobes of the brain grow measurably between ages 10 and 12. The gray matter in the lobes then begins to shrink as unused neuron branches are pruned. Studies such as these continue at different research centers, and a more complete understanding of what this all means is around the corner.

While this brain remodel has its rewards, getting through this time in your life can sometimes feel very complicated and you struggle to make sense of the world around you. Maybe you find yourself wondering why you're suddenly so concerned about what others think. Maybe you find yourself wanting more privacy. Or maybe you're just trying to understand why you have to learn algebra!

New questions. New school. New styles. You're changing. Your friends are changing. But you might be able to make more sense of these changes if you have the right information.

I'm not talking about the flood of information on cable TV, radio, or the bijillion blogs and websites on the net. I'm talking about "big picture" information about what it means to be **you**: a human being. Information so fundamental, we often forget to teach you about it in school. For example, what psychologists know about how we see, think, and feel. How these abilities work, how they change, grow or get stuck and how reliable they are as we try to make sense of ourselves, our friends, our relatives and the world around us. There is good, solid information readily available and scientifically validated, but a lot of people seem to be too busy to pay attention to it. It's like an open secret. And it's all about you...and me.

So, the next time you feel like you are struggling to crawl out from under the rubble of your remodeling, try to remember how great it's going to be when it is all done. Better yet, take an active role. Use the open secrets discovered in this book and others in this "All About Me" series as your hammer and nails to build the you that you choose to be.

In the meantime, enjoy this journey — it's all about you!

Robert Ornstein, Ph.D.
President, ISHK

Introducing:
The Cast

The concepts in this book just can't be described without some fun visuals, and so here are the little robots who'll be your guides on your journey through our discussions on memory...

The Decider and Experiences Bots

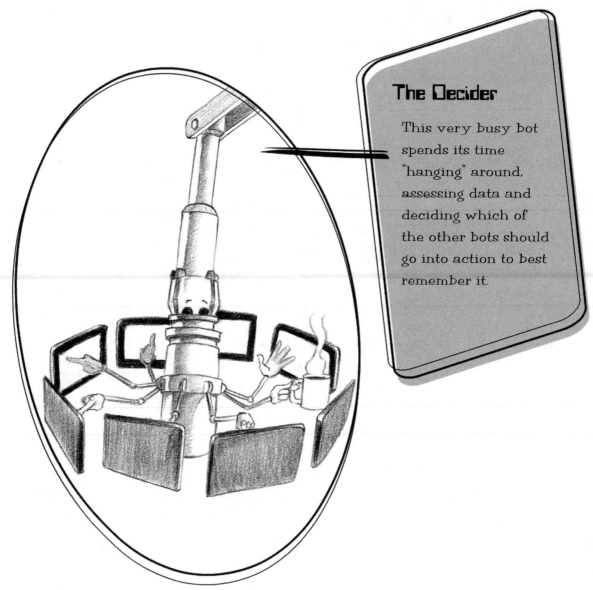

The Decider

This very busy bot spends its time "hanging" around, assessing data and deciding which of the other bots should go into action to best remember it.

Experiences Bots

These nameless bots may all look the same but each is ready to put their own emotional spin on building a memory. These ubiquitous little robots are here to laugh, cry, scowl or otherwise emote with abandon. They enjoy sunsets, sugar cookies, puppies, warm socks, dance music, and explosions.

The Cast Continued: Fact Bots

Fluffy This slow-moving fellow is the taster of the Fact Bots. With its mouth perpetually open, it's always ready to try new flavors, help to remember old ones or just eat kibble.

Otto The "sniffer" bot. With its nose to the grindstone, this nervous little machine can smell the difference between chocolate milk and regular or just let you know if it's past the due date.

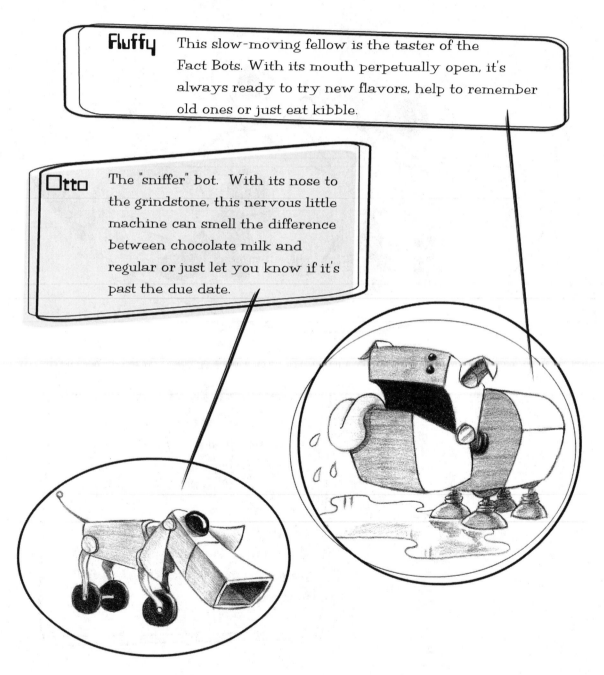

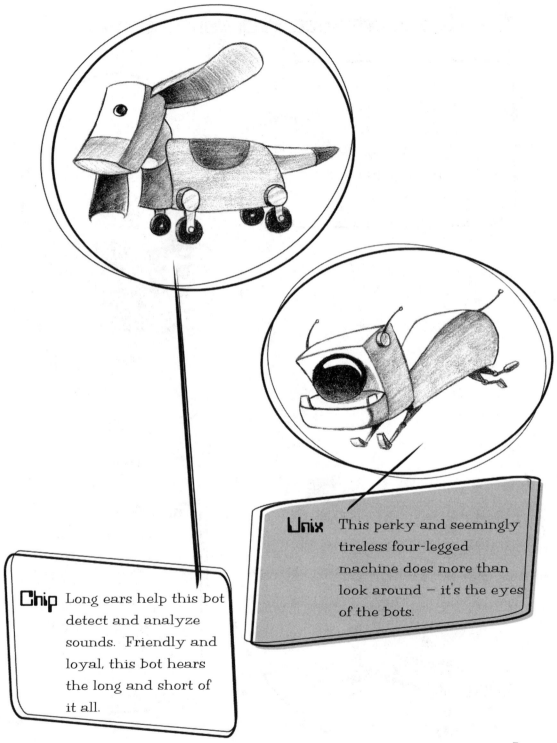

Chip Long ears help this bot detect and analyze sounds. Friendly and loyal, this bot hears the long and short of it all.

Unix This perky and seemingly tireless four-legged machine does more than look around — it's the eyes of the bots.

The Cast Continued: Procedural Bots

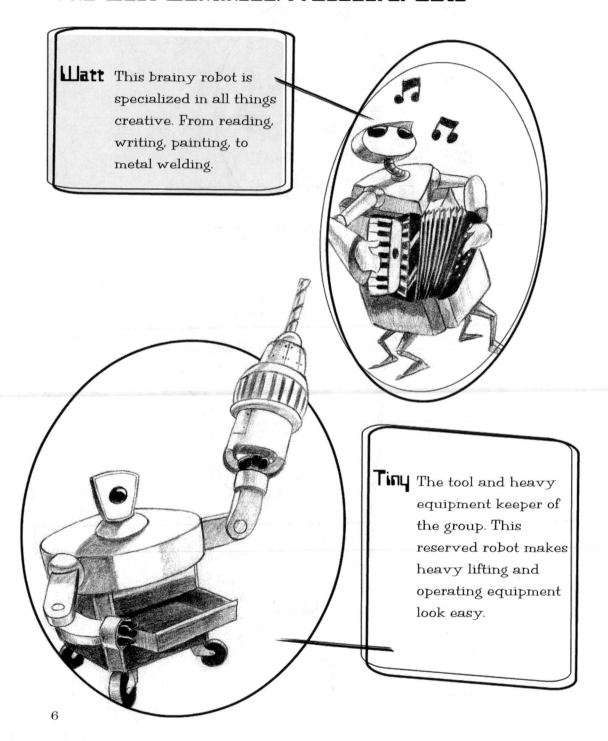

Watt This brainy robot is specialized in all things creative. From reading, writing, painting, to metal welding.

Tiny The tool and heavy equipment keeper of the group. This reserved robot makes heavy lifting and operating equipment look easy.

Shot This sporty machine is the athlete of the group. The one to rely on for all of your ball-throwing, bike-riding, log-rolling, and hoop-shooting needs.

Glot Always a wizard in the kitchen, this rolly-polly bot just loves to prepare dishes of all sorts. From couscous to cheese sandwiches, Glot is an entire kitchen on wheels.

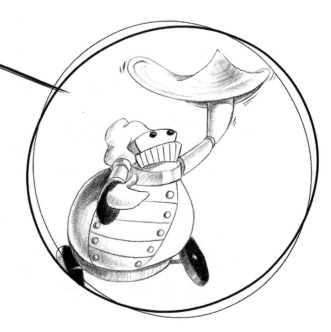

 Introduction

- You have studied for the exam, and you come to a question that you know you should know, but the answer doesn't come. You can almost sense it hovering in an inner fog, but nothing emerges. You leave the exam question blank or make a wild guess. After the exam, as you walk away, thinking of something else, the answer pops into your mind.

- You see a good friend walking toward you, but when you go to say "hi" you block on your friend's name.

- You try to recall what you had for lunch two days ago and just can't remember, but you remember a distressful event from kindergarten with striking clarity.

- It's spring. You haven't biked for six months, but when you get on the bike you ride off without a hitch.

- You and a friend both have clear memories of what people said and did at the last school dance, but your memories don't agree, so you begin to argue. Who is right?

Remembering and forgetting are complex, but important, operations. To live and function, we must be able to remember lots of stuff — who our friends are, where our home is, how to walk, how to speak English, even who we are.

Try This...

Take a moment to recall your earliest memory. Some people remember a family trip; others remember getting a special present or having a favorite person come for a visit. What do you remember?

When you're done with your earliest memory, jot down a few other "highlights" from your past. Maybe you remember the first day of first grade. Maybe you remember how you spent your summer vacations. List a few memories that take you all the way from your earliest recollections up to the present.

What's Going On?

Our memories give meaning to our life. They connect our past with our present. Our memories influence how we see ourselves, and they help shape how we will respond to new experiences and people.

We are beginning to understand more about how memory works and how it fails to work. We are learning about things that are likely to improve our memory and things that are likely to degrade it; however, there are many unanswered questions.

 Your Turn

Ask an older relative, a parent, aunt or uncle, to put on a favorite song from the past for the two of you to listen to: choose one the person hasn't listened to in a very long time. When the song is over, ask the person to share some memories that came up while the song was playing. Most people will be surprised at how much they remember about people, places and things they haven't thought about for a long time. If they have the time, have the person play a few more old songs. Get ready for a stroll down memory lane! You may find out some interesting things you never knew before about someone close to you.

In this book, we'll explore the mystery of our minds and memory. How do we remember? And how do we forget? We'll discover all that scientists and researchers know and explore the questions yet to be answered.

You will probably begin to notice how your own and other people's memories work. You will learn to understand why memory is powerful but not perfect, and you will uncover some strategies for improving your memory.

In order to get the most out of this book, you should participate in the activities along the way. Take your time. After all, what's the point in rushing to get to the last page of the book if you don't remember what you've just read!

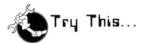 What Kinds of Memory Do We Have?

Try This...

Read the following and imagine that you are the person telling the story:

> This morning a woman came to see me in my room. I felt attracted to her. She was very pretty, and I liked talking to her. I asked her for her name. "Ellen," she said. I asked why she had come to visit me: I thought she was a hospital volunteer.
>
> She burst into tears, saying, "I'm your wife. We've been married for 20 years!"
>
> I just didn't know what to say. I don't remember her at all.

What's Going On?

The above is not fiction — a made-up story. It is a retelling of a real conversation between a man suffering from amnesia (loss of memory) and his wife of twenty years. It seems that he has forgotten everything, but has he? Notice he was able to retell or remember this conversation. There is much more that he remembered: To tell this story, he had to be able to remember English, and he had to understand what concepts like marriage and wife meant. This example points to a key fact: There is not a single type of memory in the human mind. People suffering from amnesia may forget some important details, but they still remember a lot of other stuff.

 Your Turn

Write a short conversation like the one above between you and a relative or friend. Make believe that you don't remember that person. When you are done, go back and review what you wrote. Make a list of all that you did remember.

 **More Fun**

Go to your local library or video store and check out one of the following DVDs: *The Notebook* (PG-13), *The Bourne Identity* (PG-13), *The Blue Dahlia* (1946 classic), or *50 First Dates* (PG-13). (Check with your parent or guardian before checking out any DVD to make sure it's okay with them.) These films feature characters who are suffering from memory loss. Not all of the characters have amnesia. There are many illnesses that can cause memory loss. We'll be looking at some of these conditions in Chapter 6.

People who study memory have identified a number of different kinds of memory. In our everyday conversations when we talk about "our memory," we may actually be referring to different types of memory. We will examine these different kinds of memory, individually, to get a better idea of how our memory works.

Facts and Experiences Memory

Try This...

Take out a stopwatch, or a watch with a seconds counter, and see how long it takes you to write down your answers to these questions. Or ask someone to time you. Begin the timing after reading the question and stop the timing after you write your answer. Write down the time. Be sure to include the time you spend thinking about your answer as well as the time you spend writing it down.

1) What is the capital of the United States?

2) What is your address?

3) What is your telephone number?

4) Who is the President of the United States?

Now do the same for these questions:

1) What did you do after school yesterday (or the last day you had school)?

2) What did you buy the last time you went shopping?

3) How do you celebrate on your favorite holiday?

4) What is the last song you heard?

Like most people, it probably took you longer to answer the second set of questions than the first.

What's Going On?

When you answered the first set of questions, you probably used just a word or two, enough to give the facts. You were using your **facts memory.** That's your knowledge: the facts, concepts, and language you know (including the shape of letters and the meaning of words). In your facts memory you have all the things you've learned since you were born, and it is independent of time and space. Facts memory is our **representational memory**.

When you answered the second set of questions, you probably recalled and gave a story about some episode in your life. You were using your **experiences memory.** That's the collection of individual experiences you remember — a movie, a hike in the woods, a certain book, and experiences shared with others. In contrast to your facts memory, your experiences memory is connected with particular times, places, and people. It is your store of stories.

🔎 Did You Know?

Our quantity of facts knowledge is vast; the average college student has a vocabulary of about 50,000 words in facts memory, along with the knowledge of how to combine those words properly, how to write them, and how to speak them.

Of course, experiences memory and facts memory are related. When you drew on your experiences memory to answer the question about what you did after school yesterday, you used words and concepts that were stored in your facts memory. And when you drew on your facts memory to answer questions about your address or telephone number, you could quickly have told the story of how you came to live where you do now, of how long you've been there, and so on. Stories are full of facts, and facts are surrounded by stories. Sometimes the two types may be tightly linked.

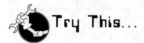

Try This...

Answer the following questions:

1) Did you ever climb a tree when you were younger?

2) Did you ever swim in a pool or in the ocean?

3) What's the farthest you have ever been from home?

What's Going On?

You're using your experiences and facts memory skills again. You could probably quickly answer either yes or no. But when you did answer, were you just stating a fact (from facts memory), like your address? Or did you perhaps have a fleeting memory of climbing a tree, meaning that you were also using your experiences memory?

Experiences and facts memory share a key feature: both involve information that we can talk about. You answered both sets of questions. For that reason, facts and experiences memories together are called **declarative memory.** We can declare or speak about these memories.

Did You Know?

Researchers have demonstrated that our experiences memory could be very precise. They asked students the question, "What were you doing on Monday afternoon in the third week of September two years ago?" The following is an example of an exchange between a subject and an experimenter:

Subject: Come on. How should I know?
Experimenter: Just try it anyhow.
Subject: Okay. Let's see, two years ago…I would have been in high school in Pittsburgh…That would be my senior year. Third week in September – that would be fall term…let me see. I think I had chemistry lab on Mondays. I don't know. I was probably in chemistry lab. Wait a minute – that would be the second week of school. I remember he started off with the atomic table – a big fancy chart. I thought he was crazy trying to make us memorize that thing. You know, I think I can remember sitting…

More Fun

Try to answer the above research question yourself. When you're done, ask a friend. Be a little persistent. Most people may assume they can't remember, but research has shown that specific experiences memories can last a long time, sometimes for decades.

Memory for Procedures

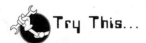 Try This…

It's time to get physical. Get up! Try one of these activities before reading on:

1) go ride a bicycle, or **2)** go bounce a ball, or **3)** time how fast it takes you to walk around your block.

If it is a nice day outside, do all three! If you can't get outside right now, try timing yourself to see how fast you can tie your shoes or button and unbutton a jacket.

What's Going On?

All of the above activities are examples of actions that are based on **procedural memory**. These memories allow us to perform the routine actions of our everyday life – whether it is getting dressed in the morning, eating lunch in the afternoon, or playing computer games. The actions can be simple like throwing a baseball or complex like writing neatly for a school assignment. This memory guides our movements in space.

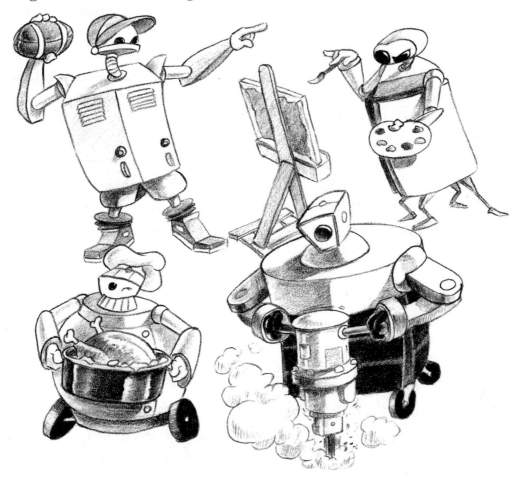

Procedural memory is sometimes referred to as "body" memory. It's the memory we rely on in order to play sports. When we learn how to make a shot in basketball, we have learned which muscle movements to make.

Practice reinforces the complex muscle movements needed to get it just right over and over again. Procedural memory is a nonverbal memory. It isn't easy to talk about it. Try explaining to someone how you balance on a bike or hit a baseball. This is one reason why a popular athletic equipment company has adopted the expression "Just Do It" as their trademark. Complex body memories are done, not spoken about. That's why Little League coaches all over the world try to get their players not to think too much when they are up at the plate waiting to swing the bat — especially if the player is in a slump!

Procedural memory also underlies many of our everyday perceptual experiences. We know when we are eating a turkey sandwich rather than a peanut butter and jelly sandwich. We can tell that the milk is sour or when someone is singing off key. But, can you tell someone what turkey tastes like? Or what sour is? Have you ever tried to explain to someone how to sing on key?

When we try to describe what we perceive or how we do some things, our descriptions are likely to be general, vague, or even inaccurate. Often we end up saying things like "do this" and then demonstrating the action or "taste this and then you'll know." We may not be able to describe it or explain how to do it, but we can recognize it or do it over and over again. For procedural memory, it's easier done (or perceived) than said.

Your Turn

Get a pencil, drawing pens, and paper. Pretend you are a bike-riding expert and write a "how-to" manual for non-riders. If you find it hard to put this into words, draw pictures of the steps involved. It's not as easy as it sounds, because you're trying to describe something from your procedural memory. That's the kind of memory you have of things you learned to do in a nonverbal way, that is, without words or written manuals.

More Fun

You perform countless actions everyday. Think about something you do on a regular basis and perform it slowly. For example, open and close a door slowly. Jot down a list of the procedures you follow to do this activity as if you had to teach it to a friend. Have a friend try and do something similar. Don't be surprised if you find it difficult to verbalize the procedure. That's just the way procedural memory works.

Memory for Specific Facts

Try This...

Read the list on the next page. Then put the items in order to show where your memory is strongest and where it is weakest. Make number one the area where you think your memory is strongest and number eight the area that is weakest (1 = strongest; 8 = weakest). There are no right or wrong answers.

Different people will order the items in different ways.

- ☐ Remembering such things as numbers and addresses without having to recheck them.
- ☐ Remembering what you just did or were intending to do.
- ☐ Remembering people's names.
- ☐ Recognizing people by their appearance.
- ☐ Remembering jokes, stories, and conversations.
- ☐ Remembering your to-do list.
- ☐ Remembering or recalling why something seems familiar.
- ☐ Remembering where things are.

What's Going On?

Declarative memory (facts or experiences: those you can talk about) and procedural memory (nonverbal) are still fairly general. It may be that we remember different kinds of things in different ways. One kind of evidence for this is that different people seem to have differing strengths and weaknesses in remembering. Teachers may remember specific details of the American Revolutionary War or the structures of a plant cell but forget to bring their students' graded tests back to school. One person may have a good memory for faces but not for numbers, while another remembers numbers but can't remember faces. One person may have a great memory for jokes and names but forget to do everyday things.

Two psychologists, Hermann and Neisser, developed a questionnaire called the Inventory of Memory Experiences (IME). The IME asked people how well they remembered the same things you were asked to order in the above activity. The results suggested that our memories are organized around at least eight types of experiences or tasks:

1) **Rote memory** - Remembering or forgetting such things as numbers and addresses without having to recheck them.

2) **Absentmindedness** - Forgetting what one has just done or intended to do.

3) **Names** - The ability or inability to recall people's names.

4) **People** - Recognizing individuals by their appearance.

5) **Conversation** - Remembering jokes, stories, and conversations.

6) **Errands** - Remembering things to do.

7) **Retrieval** - Ability or inability to recall why something seems familiar.

8) **Place** - Remembering where things are.

Memory for Procedures

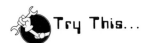 Try This...

Answer as many of these questions as you can:
1) Which organ is part of the digestive system?
2) What does a plant cell contain that an animal cell does not?
3) What is one hundred divided by four?

Now try to answer these questions:

1) Which organ is not part of the digestive system?
    (A) the stomach, (B) the large intestine, (C) the small intestine, (D) the heart
2) Which is contained in a plant cell only?
    (A) nucleus, (B) chlorophyll, (C) cytoplasm, (D) cell membrane
3) What is one hundred divided by four?
    (A) 30, (B) 50, (C) 25, (D) 20

What's Going On?

Memory can also be classified by depth or the kind of use we can make of it. **Recognition**, knowing that you have experienced or seen something before, is a different type of memory from **recall**, which involves actively trying to remember something. You may, for example, recognize a book when you look at it but not recall what it is about. Or you may recognize a person but not be able to recall who the person is. Or you may be able to answer a multiple-choice question correctly on a test (recognition), but not be able to produce the answer to an open-ended question (recall). You may be able to remember a rule in math but not remember how to use it to solve a problem. Or you may be able to use the math rule yourself but not be able to explain it to your friend. You may be able to see a dance step or a basketball dunk shot clearly in your mind but not be able to do the dance or dunk the ball.

Some information is easy for you to recall: your name, your birthday, and your phone number. Other information can be more difficult for you to recall: directions to a friend's house or the address of your school. Information you learn in school can be especially difficult for you to recall.

It is easier to recognize something than to recall it. You may have noticed that it is often easier for a teacher from your past to recognize you than to recall your name! Multiple-choice tests are easier than those that require you to produce the answer. That's why you may have found the second set of questions above easier than the first. Recognition is easier because something is present, a stimulus, that can call up the matching memory.

⏻ Did You Know?

The capacity of our recognition memory is huge. In one study, researchers showed subjects 2,560 photos for 10 seconds each. A few days later, the subjects' recognition of the photos was greater than 90 percent. In other words, they could correctly identify over 2,304 photos!

Sense Memory

🔧 Try This...

Look through your kitchen for a favorite treat. When you find one, close your eyes and smell it. Enjoy the smell. Write down a pleasant experience associated with this smell. Maybe it was the first time you ever ate this treat or maybe it was the time you brought it along on a trip with your family or friends.

What's Going On?

Our memories also seem to vary depending on what sense (smell, sight, sound, and touch) is involved. Smell is one of our oldest and most basic senses, so an important component of real-world memories is odor. French writer, Marcel Proust, in a famous passage from his novel *Swann's Way*, describes how the smell of madeleine cookies summoned up details of his childhood.

Brown University has a collection of more than 100 different odors, ranging from a skunk's scent to the scent of whiskey. In one experiment, people sniffed 48 cotton balls, each saturated with a different odor. Afterward, a second group of odors was presented, including many from the first group, and 69% of the odors were recognized as having been in the first group. While this is a very high rate of remembering, it is not as high as people's rate when they are asked if they have seen images before. However, the rate of forgetting odors seems slower. In the Brown University study, people were able to recognize 70% of the odors after

GAK!

one week and 68% one month later. We also have an enormous capacity in recognition memory for pictures. One study selected 612 familiar pictures and allowed people to review slides of the pictures at their own pace. Immediately afterward, the people were shown pictures and asked to say if they had reviewed them or not. They were able to recognize almost 97% of the pictures they had reviewed. In fact, when they were asked again after four months had passed, the people could still recognize more than 50% of the pictures.

Your Turn

Design an activity to demonstrate the power of your sense memory with family or friends. Here are a couple of suggestions:

- Collect several household, food, or bathroom products. See if you can get the same results as the Brown University experiment. Check with an adult before inhaling any product other than a food item. Many household products can be unsafe to breath.

- Look around the house for an old photo album or high-school yearbook. If the yearbook belongs to a parent or guardian, go through the book and have the person identify as many people as possible. If it's an old family photo album that you haven't looked at in years, see how many people you recognize. Wedding albums can be fun for this activity.

Time and Duration

Try This...

Stare at a clock for five minutes. Don't do anything. Just stare at it. When you are finished, spend another five minutes on this activity, but this time I want you to do something – anything. You can listen to music, watch TV, talk on the phone, or even clean your room!

When you are done with both, think about which five minutes "felt" longer. Sure they were both five minutes, but I bet the first activity felt like a lot more than five minutes when compared to the second. Were you even able just to stare at the clock for the full five minutes? If you are like most people you may have had a difficult time.

What's Going On?

We use our eyes to see and our ears to hear, but we don't have a sensory organ for the experience of time. If you wait an hour with nothing to do, it may seem like an eternity. This is why your parents will often tell you to do something instead of just sitting around. And this is why people try to find ways to preoccupy themselves on long car trips. One popular game is to keep track of license plates until you have recorded at least one plate from all of the fifty states. This is not as easy as it sounds, but it's a good way to make time seem to go faster.

Although an hour may seem like an eternity while you are waiting, in the long run, you will probably not even remember that hour! Researchers have discovered that the fewer the number of events in a given time, the shorter the time will seem when you remember it later. A boring car trip will probably disappear from your memory and, in retrospect, seem quite short.

The more we remember of a given situation, the longer it seems. For example, we experience a piece of music that contains 40 sounds per minute as shorter than one with 80 per minute. We judge time past by how much we remember. This is why vacations seem so long.

If you are on an interesting vacation, each day is filled with new experiences, people, and places. At the end of a couple of weeks, it seems as if you have been on vacation forever. When you return home, at first your memories and descriptions of the experience are quite complex: "We went to Waikiki Beach and swam, snorkeled at Hanama Bay beach, got surfing lessons, stayed at a hotel with three swimming pools." Later, memory may change. It may be simply, "I went to Hawaii for two weeks last year and had a great time."

Familiar experiences, such as driving a car through an area you know well, seem shorter than the same amount of time in unfamiliar territory. This is why it often seems to take longer to get to someplace than it does to return home.

Long-Term and Short-Term Memory

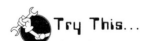 Try This...

Find a phone book and choose a telephone number at random. If you can't find a phone book, ask a parent or guardian for an unfamiliar number. Repeat the number once to yourself, but don't write it down. Now go find pen and paper and write down several phone numbers that you know. While you're at it, jot down your address and the address of your school. After you have done all this, try to write down the unfamiliar number.

Were you able to remember the unfamiliar number? Did you only remember part of it? Don't be surprised if you didn't remember any of it! Unless you have a good rote memory you probably had difficulty remembering this new number.

What's Going On?

Sometimes we think of memory in terms of time. We refer to **short-term memory** and **long-term memory**. Information that is retained temporarily, for only a few seconds, is stored in short-term memory. When you look up a phone number, you have to remember the number only long enough to dial it. If you encounter interference, that is, if something distracts you, you may have to look the number up again. For example, if you get a busy signal or someone talks to you, you are likely to forget the number. To get information from short-term memory into long-term memory, you need to make an effort to learn it.

You do not have to look up your own telephone number when you call home, nor do you have to recite your name over and over to remember it. Both experiences and facts memories are long-term memories. Of course, there are different kinds of long-term memory. You might study a definition for a science test and remember it for a day or two and then forget it, while other memories might remain clear and strong for years.

Your Turn

Test out the effects of interference on short-term memory for yourself. You'll need to find a partner for this activity; someone who won't mind being distracted by you.

First, you will need an inflated balloon or something else that will make a sharp noise. You can clap your hands if you can't find something to use. Don't tell your partner that you are going to make the noise. For the experiment to work, the noise needs to be a surprise. Ask your partner to choose a phone number at random and memorize it. After about 10 seconds, make the noise. Then ask the person to recite the phone number. Be sure to explain the reason for the experiment: that you're learning how easy it is to forget something that is only in short-term memory.

Test Your Memory on Chapter 2

Instructions: Fill in the blanks with answers.

1. The two main categories of memory are _____ and
_____.

2. _____ memory includes experiences memory and facts
memory.

3. _____ is the store of our individual experiences.
It has been called an "autobiographical reference." These memories
are precise and constantly being updated.

4. Facts memory stores our knowledge of language: symbols, sounds,
and meanings. This memory is independent of time and space.
Facts memory also contains the rules that allow us to make com-
monsense, everyday inferences. Facts memory is our
_____ memory.

5. Procedural memory is the nonverbal memory. It allows us to
perform routine actions. These actions may be simple or complex.
Procedural memory is sometimes called _____ memory.

6. Research suggests that memory can be organized around other
types of experience or tasks: rote memory, absentmindedness,
_____, people, conversation, errands, retrieval, and _____.
Different people are better at different types.

7. Recognition and recall are often tested in school. _____
can help with multiple-choice questions; however, only _____ can
help you with short answers and essays.

8. Our memories seem to vary depending on what sense is
involved. _____ and _____ seem to stimulate the most memories.

9. Our memories of time or duration vary. The _____ number of
events in a given time, the shorter it will seem when we remember
it later on. Activity-packed days will be remembered as being
longer.

10. Short-term and _____ refer to how long information is
retained. Short-term memories are only retained for a few seconds
and are quickly forgotten if interfered with.

Keep It In Mind

School requires learners to use their memory daily. One effective strategy for helping learners remember what they are learning is called **SQ3R.**

S is for Survey. Survey or look over a text before reading it to get an idea about what you will be reading.

Q is for Question. Turn headings into questions. These questions will guide your reading. For example, if the heading is "Long-Term and Short-Term Memory," you could write down the question "What is the difference between long-term and short-term memory?"

3R is for Read, Recite, and Review. For each section that you have written a question, read that section for the answer to your question. When you have answered your question, recite what you have learned. When you have answered all your questions, review all that you have learned.

Reviewing is an important part of improving long-term memory. Follow the Rule of Five when reviewing: Review your notes (1) one hour later, (2) one day later, (3) one week later, (4) one month later, and 5) three months later. Regular reviewing will help keep the new information in your memory.

Answers for Chapter Two

1. declarative and procedural, 2. Declarative, 3. Experiences memory, 4. representational, 5. body, 6. names, place, 7. Recognition, recall, 8. Sight and smell, 9. fewer, 10. long-term

How Does Memory Work?

Memory is complex. Not only are there many different kinds of memories, there are also several different ways of understanding how memory works. We will examine each of these ways of understanding how memories are made and lost individually to help us understand memory and forgetting as a whole.

The Memory Cycle

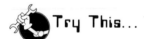 Try This...

Think back to your studies of science. Do you remember learning about the water cycle. Look at the diagram below which shows the main processes in this cycle. As you can see, when the

The Water Cycle

air near the earth's surface is warmed, it causes the water on the surface to evaporate. As the warm air rises, it carries the evaporated moisture upward. Higher up, as the temperature cools, the water in the air condenses. This condensation falls back to earth as precipitation (rain, hail, snow). The main parts of this cycle are: evaporation, condensation, and precipitation. You'll use your understanding of this as you learn about the memory cycle.

What's Going On?

The memory cycle has three main parts: perception, storage, and retrieval. To remember something, you first have to **perceive** it. The information must be picked up by your senses, which then relay it to your brain. Once in your brain, the information must be **stored**. The storage time may be a few seconds, a few years, or an entire lifetime.

Think again about what happens when you cram for a test. Occasionally, you try to direct what you remember consciously. For example, you say to yourself, "I am going to remember that word." But usually your brain just unconsciously selects things on the basis of some simple "rules." For example, your brain follows the rules *remember an experience that is striking or new, remember things related to my interests or what is important to my life,* or *store information related to other stored memories,* and so on.

The third part of the memory cycle is **retrieval.** For a memory to be brought into your consciousness, you have to retrieve the stored information. In the last section, you learned about two types of retrieval — recognition and recall. As you'll remember, it is easier to recognize something that is in front of you (multiple-choice options, for instance) than to have to recall it.

The memory cycle has been compared to a filing cabinet or to a computer hard drive, tools we use to store information. Once information is stored in a filing cabinet or a computer's memory, the user can retrieve it when needed.

PERCEPTION

Your Turn

Can you think of any other cycles that you can compare to the memory cycle? Think beyond examples you may have come across in science class. What other cycles are you familiar with? One student came up with the "dressing" cycle: putting clothes on, wearing clothes, and taking clothes off. See if you can think of other examples from your daily life.

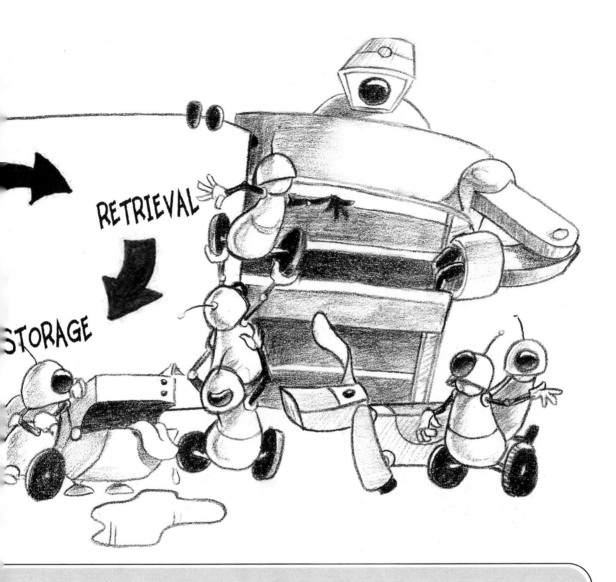

RETRIEVAL

STORAGE

Can you think of any other storage devices or storage systems to compare to the memory cycle? Think about some of the latest high-tech gadgets available. To think of comparisons, start by thinking about libraries or warehouses.

Memory as a Change Resulting from Experience

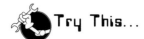 Try This...

Create a canyon outside. You can try this anywhere with a little sand or dirt to play in. You can also create this in a couple of buckets. All you need to do is slowly pour a glass of water through a small area of sand or dirt. Notice how the water creates a small channel. Repeat this process for a few times and you will notice that this channel gets deeper and deeper with each glass of water

you pour into it, and the water flows easier and faster through the channel. If you have a few drain downspouts that carry the water from the roof of your house or apartment and these spouts empty into dirt, you may notice that over time ruts are created in front of these spouts.

What's Going On?

The memory cycle described in the last section is only one theory of how our memory works. Another theory suggests that our experiences cause physical changes to our brain and that these changes are what we call "memories." To understand this, think about what happens to a person's body during exercise. With exercise, muscles change shape and change their ability to perform. Some people think that "memory" involves similar changes in the brain. They say that after a certain experience we are more likely to act differently or speak differently.

People who think experience affects memory focus on the nerve cells in the brain. Our brain has networks of nerve cells. Each experience may activate a specific track in this network, and each time a track is activated, it may become easier for the nerve cells along that track to become active again. In the same way that water carves out a canyon, and once a path is created, it becomes much easier for water to travel the same way. This may explain why people so easily make the same mistake over and over again. It may also explain why habits are so easy to pick up and so hard to break.

Your Turn

Think about your own behavior. Have you ever tried to change a habit but couldn't seem do it? Did your behavior seem to follow a well-worn path? Consider your eating habits. Do you drink soft drinks or eat "junk food"? Why not try breaking that habit? Be prepared for some difficulty as you try to "dig a new path."

Memory as a Construction

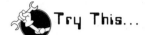Try This...

Look at the following illustration titled "Portrait d'Homme." These drawings were made from memory in an unusual way. The person who drew Reproduction 1 looked at the original drawing for a short time and then drew it from memory; the person who drew Reproduction 2 looked only at Reproduction 1 and drew it from

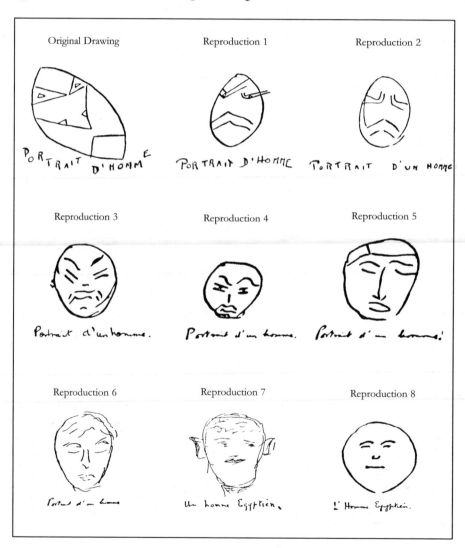

memory; the person who drew Reproduction 3 had looked only at Reproduction 2 and drew it from memory, and so on. What do you notice as you study the drawings? What do they suggest to you about how memory works?

What's Going On?

In 1932, Frederic Bartlett wrote an important book on remembering that was based on his experiments. He thought that when we remember something, we don't just retrieve the information from our mental storage system, but actually we build the memory, or **construct** it.

One method he used in his experiments is similar to the game "telephone." A person is given a drawing and asked to reproduce it from memory. That person then presents his or her reproduction to the next person, who reproduces it, and so on. Bartlett called this method **serial reproduction**. Bartlett also asked people to reproduce drawings repeatedly over time, and he called this the **method of repeated reproduction.**

Bartlett deliberately chose drawings that were unfamiliar to residents of Cambridge, England, where he did his research. The illustration on the previous page is one example of serial reproduction, a series of drawings that begin with an original African drawing, "Portrait d'Homme." In these drawings, the subjects transformed figures to look like familiar figures that were already in their memories. According to Dr. Bartlett, people have a tendency to transform odd or unfamiliar figures into conventional or familiar ones. In each successive reproduction of the African drawing, the original unconventional features are dropped. The final figure is an ordinary representation of a face. It is interesting, however, that the exotic qualities of the original drawing's title are retained in the changes the subjects made to the title.

Your Turn

Bartlett conducted his experiments with stories as well as drawings. People would read or be told a story and then write down or retell that story. Here is an example of one of the stories

Bartlett used. It is a Native American folk story. Read it once to yourself and then, without looking at the text again, write the story, making it as close to the original as you can. When you finish, read how two of Bartlett's English students wrote out this tale.

Here is the original story:

The War of the Ghosts

One night two young men from Egulac went down to the river to hunt seals, and while they were there it became foggy and calm. Then they heard war-cries, and they thought: "Maybe this is a war-party." They escaped to the shore, and hid behind a log. Now canoes came up, and they heard the noise of the paddle, and saw one canoe coming up to them. There were five men in the canoe, and they said: "What do you think? We wish to take you along. We are going up the river to make war on the people." One of the young men said: "I have no arrows." "Arrows are in the canoe," they said. "I will not go along. I might be killed. My relatives do not know where I have gone. But you," he said, turning to the other, "may go with them." So one of the young men went, but the other returned home. And the warriors went on up the river to a town on the other side of Kalama. The people came down to the water, and they began to fight, and many were killed. But presently the young man heard one of the warriors say: "Quick, let us go home: that Indian has been hit." Now he thought: "Oh, they are ghosts." He did not feel sick, but they said he had been shot. So the canoes went back to Egulac, and the young man went ashore to his house, and made a fire. And he told everybody and said: "Behold, I accompanied the ghosts, and we went to fight. Many of our fellows were killed, and many of those who attacked us were killed. They said I was hit, and I did not feel sick." He told it all, and then he became quiet. When the sun rose he fell down. Something black came out of his mouth. His face became contorted. The people jumped up and cried. He was dead.

Now, before you read on, close the book and write this story from memory. If you like, show what you wrote to a friend or relative and have that person write it down from memory. Then you will experience serial reproduction firsthand.

Here is an example of the result of serial reproduction from Bartlett's experiment. This story was reproduced by the eighth person in the chain:

> Two Indians from Momapan were fishing for seals when a boat came along containing five warriors. "Come with us," they said to the Indians, "and help us to fight the warriors further on." The first Indian replied: "I have a mother at home, and she would grieve greatly if I were not to return." The other Indian said, "I have no weapons." "We have some in the boat," said the warriors. The Indian stepped into the boat. In the course of the fight further on, the Indian was mortally wounded, and his spirit fled. "Take me to my home," he said, "at Momapan, for I am going to die." "No, you will not die," said a warrior. In spite of this, however, he died, and before he could be carried back to the boat, his spirit had left this world.

Notice that the English student transformed the story into a more conventional one. The original Native American names are gone, although "Momapan" has been added. Native American cultural themes disappear or are replaced by English ones. For example, canoes become boats and references to ghosts are gone. The story becomes more and more simple with each retelling. Here is another version of the story by a person who had read the original six months earlier:

> Four men came down to the water. They were told to get into a boat and to take arms with them. They inquired, "What arms?" and were answered, "Arms for battle." When they came to the battlefield, they heard a great noise and shouting and a voice said, "The black man is dead." And he was brought to the place where they were and laid on the ground. And he foamed at the mouth.

Notice, again, how much of the detail is gone from this story and how the unfamiliar terms have again been lost. The ghosts are gone. The unusual reference in the original story to something black coming from the dying man's mouth has been transformed into a black man who dies, foaming at the mouth.

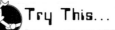

More Fun

Create your own experiments to demonstrate serial reproduction and show how our memories seem not just to be retrieved but to be constructed. You can start by assembling a group of friends or relatives and playing the telephone game. In this game, people sit in a circle. One person thinks of something interesting to say (a sentence or two), writes it down, and whispers it to the next person in the circle. That person whispers the information to the next person, and so on, until it's the last person's turn. That person then says aloud the information, and the first person reads what's on the paper. The group can then see how much the information has changed by the time it gets to the last person. For something more challenging, choose an unfamiliar drawing or a brief article from a newspaper or magazine to use for the serial reproduction.

What happened in your experiment? Can you identify how the unfamiliar was transformed into something more familiar? What other interesting results do you notice?

Memory as a Cultural System

Try This...

Consider what can happen on a popular television game show. A contestant will win a lot of money by answering just one more question correctly. The person doesn't know the answer, but has the chance to poll the audience, call a friend, or even ask a stranger for help. The person gets help from the audience and wins!

Now, compare that situation with the next one. The following excerpt is from an article on the Moken people of South Surin Island, Thailand. It was written by Abby Goodnough for the International Herald Tribune shortly after a tsunami in December 2004 killed thousands of people. As you read, think about what this situation has in common with the game show.

South Surin Island, Thailand: They call it "wave that eats people," but the Moken, who have lived in isolation here for decades, emerged from the tsunami almost unscathed. About 200 Moken were living on South Surin Island, 65 kilometers, or 40 miles, from Thailand's shore, when the wave hit on Dec. 26 as it was barreling toward the coast. Their village, built of thatched huts on stilts, was on the beach. But when the water crashed over it, the Moken, including old women and parents with babies on their backs, had already run to the hills.

The Moken know the mysteries of the ocean better than most Thais, having roamed it for centuries as fishermen and divers. They used to live half the year in houseboats on the Andaman Sea, wandering between Thailand and Myanmar; and, while less itinerant now, they remain closely attuned to the water. They are animists who believe that the sea, their island and all objects have spirits, and the Moken use totem poles to communicate with them.

Salama Klathalay, chief of the Moken here, said his elders had taught him to expect a people-eating wave whenever the tide receded far and fast. So when he witnessed such a sight on the morning of Dec. 26, he started running and shouting. "I had never seen such a low tide," said Salama, a lively white-haired man who said he was at least 60 but unsure of his exact age. "I started telling people that a wave was coming."*

While these two scenarios (the game show and the tsunami stories) are dramatically different, they have something in common: it's the kind of memory that is being relied on. Let's explore this further.

---

*You can find a complete version of the article at the weblink: http://www.burmanet.org/news/2005/01/24/the-international-herald-tribune-how-a-tribe-of-thai-animists-listened-to-the-sea-and-survived-abby-goodnough/

What's Going On?

The views of memory you have read about so far all focus on memory as something that happens in the individual mind. However, for tens of thousands of years, humans have also formed **cultural memories**. These are drawings, in buildings, in books, and more recently in computers. These are called **external memories** because they come from generations of human memory and learning and are available to all of us who share the culture. External memory also means that we can achieve levels of complexity that are beyond the capacity of an individual mind. Imagine a person having to know all the things needed to make and operate an airline system, to launch a satellite to Mars, to extract, process and distribute oil across the globe. We can accomplish these things only because many people have recorded what they know, and we can access those "memories" as we need them.

One kind of external memory that we depend on is **social memory**. For example, you may know that one of your friends knows a lot about music, so you go to that friend to get the name of a popular song. Another friend can give details about players for Major League Baseball teams. An older uncle or aunt may be the best source for finding out about what your mother was like when she was 12 years old. We come to know who holds the best memory for different kinds of information. You probably rely on social memory more than you realize. Whenever you ask a friend for the pages to a homework assignment or for help on a homework question, you are using one kind of social memory.

Retrieval of external memories also takes learning. An amazing amount of information is now in books in English, but you need to know English and be able to read to access these external memories. Likewise, much information is now stored in computers throughout the world that are linked on the World Wide Web, but again you need to have a computer and have learned the skills to operate one in order to access and retrieve this information.

One problem facing the modern world is the loss of the cultural memory of small communities like the Moken of South Surin Island. As more and more Moken youths join mainstream Thai society, the knowledge of their elders about the signs of the sea are being lost forever. Since the tsunami of 2004, many young Mokens now see the value in the "old-fashioned" ways of their parents and are encouraged to learn the ways of their elders so that this cultural memory is not lost to humankind. Throughout the world, many native or indigenous cultures face the same struggle. In the United States, this struggle can be seen as Native American cultures or Native Hawaiian cultures

struggle to retain the knowledge of their ancestors.

The memory in our own minds and our external cultural memories must work together. But without our minds, without our understanding, the cultural memory system would become a dead system. The author Doris Lessing has written about just such a scenario in her novels *Mara and Dann* and *The Story of General Dann and Mara's Daughter, Griot and the Snow Dog*. In these novels set in the far future, most of the world is covered in ice, and the knowledge of most technologies that we rely on today has been lost. The main characters struggle to regain the cultural memory systems lost in this futuristic Ice Age. While the shells of airplanes still exist, people don't know how to fly them or even power them up. Instead the planes are hitched to animals and transport people like stagecoaches of the Old West.

Your Turn

Get a firsthand experience of just how much we rely on the cultural memory and on the skills of others. Walk around your apartment or house and make a list of all the items that would be useless if they broke down and could not be repaired by anyone in the household. Imagine what your life would be like if all of your most basic possessions and tools fell into disrepair.

Afterwards, make a list of as many things and places that involve some type of storage of cultural or external memories. A library is one type; a documentary film is another type.

Applying the Metaphors for Memory

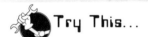

Try This...

Think about the metaphors for memory that we have been considering: memory as a computer and memory as an exercising muscle. Think of examples from your school day when you can apply these metaphors. When do you notice that you use your memory like a computer — storing and retrieving information? When do you notice that your memory is like an exercising muscle?

Consider some common situations like taking notes off the board or changing your lunchtime routine to avoid someone.

What's Going On?

Both the metaphor of memory as a computer and the metaphor of it as an exercising muscle agree that experiences change us and are reflected in our memories. They differ on the question of how those changes are reflected in memory and in the world around us.

If we accept that our culture reveals a cultural memory, then we should be able to see how our two metaphors can be applied to cultural artifacts or objects. Let's consider an object like a hammer. We can say that this object, the hammer, has been shaped by human experience (the exercise metaphor). The shape, design, and materials of the hammer hold a kind of memory of human hands and muscles as well as of our cultural practices for building. Think of another object like a chair. While the basic design of a chair has remained the same for hundreds, if not thousands, of years, there have been changes that reveal a memory of how its use has changed. In schools, student chairs have evolved into student desks – all-in-one units. In the office, the chair has evolved to include lumbar supports and height adjustments to meet the need of a workforce that has to sit for many hours a day.

The words of languages are another example of the exercise metaphor. The words of a language are shaped by thousands of years of human experience, of what is important to name and talk about in the part of the world that you live in. It is no surprise that people of the polar regions have a vocabulary rich in words to describe snow and ice while those of the Sahara have many words to describe the sands of the desert.

Other objects, such as books, notebooks, maps and, of course, the computer show the computer metaphor is present in our culture. These are objects where information can be stored and then retrieved for later use. There are many more objects that can be added to this list from filing cabinets to DVDs.

Your Turn

Try to apply the computer and exercise metaphors to other artifacts or objects in your world. Especially think about our language. How has our language changed recently to reveal the influence of new technologies? Ask an older relative to make a list of words that are used in a new way or did not exist when they were your age but which you take for granted; words such as "email," "texting," "dude," etc.

Memory and the Metaphor of the Elephant

While we examine different ways memory works, we should remember that these individual ways work together as a whole. Consider one more metaphor of how our memory works in the following story:

An elephant belonging to a traveling exhibition had been stabled near a town where no elephant had been seen before. Four curious citizens, hearing of the hidden wonder, went to see if they could get a preview of it. When they arrived at the stable they found that there was no light. The investigation therefore had to be carried out in the dark.

One, touching its trunk, thought that the creature must resemble a hose; the second felt an ear and concluded that it was a fan. The third, feeling a leg, could liken it only to a living pillar; and when the fourth put his hand on its back he was convinced it was some kind of throne. None could form the complete picture.

(Idries Shah, *The Sufis*, p. 40.)

If we are to avoid the mistakes made with the elephant in the dark, we should remember that our memory involves storing and retrieving information, as well as adapting to experience. Memory as information and as experience each represents a part of the whole. A part of memory is probably a little like a computer, storing words, phrases, and specific events that can later be retrieved. But for much of our life, we don't store exact bits of information simply because we might need them in the future. Rather, our general concern is **adaptation**: being able to change our behavior as a result of our experiences.

We learn, for example, to avoid someone who once caused us pain. Most of us will avoid the schoolyard bully. Previous experience with that person produced changes in us. We may begin to pick up information about other people who we think also cause us pain by noticing similarities between them and a person who has hurt us before. Maybe there is something about his or her behavior that reminds us of that schoolyard bully. We are not simply retrieving information. The process is far more complex. Instead, we become tuned differently; we perceive and act differently.

While the use of metaphors is helpful in understanding how memory works, we must remember that no comparison to a single machine, even a machine as complex as a computer, is sufficient to explain the complexity of the human mind.

Test Your Memory on Chapter 3

Complete the mind map.

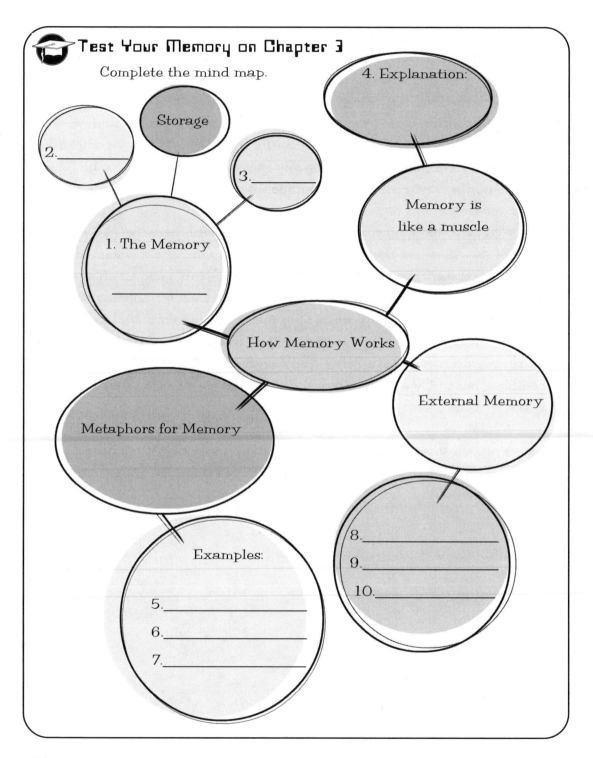

Storage

2._____

4. Explanation:

3._____

1. The Memory

_____

Memory is like a muscle

How Memory Works

External Memory

Metaphors for Memory

Examples:

5._____

6._____

7._____

8._____

9._____

10._____

Keep It In Mind

Visual tools or graphic organizers like the mind map above can be used as an alternative way of taking notes. You can also use these tools when studying. If you have taken notes in the traditional way, try rewriting them using a mind map. Below are a couple more examples you can try. Many more can be found by doing an internet search. Search keyword: "mind map" or "graphic organizer." Always check with a parent first before conducting an internet search or visiting unfamiliar web sites. (More note-taking ideas are explored in Chapter 9.)

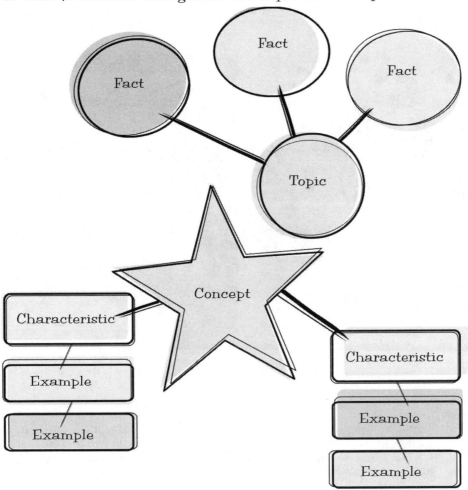

And remember, it's not just at school that we experience difficulties; maybe you're having trouble learning how to swim or how to play a musical instrument. One way to begin to improve is to develop a schedule. Set aside a regular time and place to study or practice. As mentioned in the last chapter, it takes regular review and practice to transfer information to long-term memory.

When setting aside time to study, don't overdo it. Your brain gets tired just like your muscles do. Avoid marathon or all-nighter study sessions which are not very efficient. Study for twenty to fifty minutes, then take a ten-minute break to refresh your brain.

Answers for Chapter Three
    1. cycle, 2. perception, 3. retrieval, 4. Like a muscle that changes after physical exercises, our daily experiences cause changes to the brain, and these changes are our memories. 5, 6, and 7: Answers will vary. Some suggestions: computer, filing cabinet, elephant in the dark. 8, 9, and 10: Answers will vary. Some suggestions: school, libraries, films.

Some Key Principles Of Memory

Try This...

Think about a recent memorable event and draw a picture of it. Include as many details as possible. When you have completed your drawing, make a list of the things about the day of the event that you may not remember, such as what you had for breakfast or how many people you talked to on that day.

What's Going On?

If you are like most people, your drawing is probably close to representing the actual event, but you also probably left out some details, such as those on your list. You've just seen another a key principle of memory: **Memories are much simpler than actual experience**. Too much information is available for us to remember it all. How many of the millions of moments you lived last summer do you remember? You remember some days well – perhaps a wonderful day of swimming, some fine days spent with friends, etc. – but you don't remember the weather on any random day, or how many birds you saw on that day, or how many times your friend said "like" or "dude" yesterday.

Try This...

Without looking at a real quarter, try to tell which drawing is an accurate representation of a quarter.

What's Going On?

You may have found this harder than you first thought. This activity illustrates another principle: **We remember meaningful events.** We remember events that are important to us. Since we usually remember only meaningful details, we often overlook other details. Most people cannot readily tell which quarter is the real one, although we see quarters daily. That's because the details on the quarter are not meaningful to us. Whether Washington faces left or right and where the date is placed don't matter to us, and we normally do not remember them, even though we see quarters thousands of times. Then again, if you're a coin collector, coins are meaningful to you, and you may have spotted the real quarter right away.

Did You Know?

The famous psychologist William James wrote about memory over a hundred years ago! He wrote:

> The more other facts a fact is associated with in the mind, the better possession of it our memory retains. Each of its associates becomes a hook on to which it hangs, a means to fish it up when sunk beneath the surface. Together they form a network of attachments by which it is woven into the tissue of our thought. The "secret of a good memory" is the secret of forming diverse and multiple associations with every fact we care to retain... Most men have a good memory for facts connected with their own pursuits... The merchant remembers prices, the politician other politicians' speeches and votes.

> — William James, *Psychology*, 1892.

Association

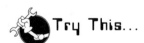

Try This...

Choose a song that was your favorite last summer or last school year. If you can, listen to that song. If not, just sing it to yourself. While you're listening to that song, write down all the memories that that song brings back. This will help illustrate a third principle: **Memory is organized around associated events.**

What's Going On?

When you think about a parent, a friend, or even a song, you recall things that relate to your knowledge of that person or song. Memories of other people and of unrelated events usually do not intrude. If memory were a random collection of bits of information, you would have to rifle through millions of memories simply to recognize a face or the voice of someone calling your name.

Think about a personal collection you may have – a DVD/CD collection, a collection of magazines or books, or, maybe, just your clothes drawers. Most of us organize this stuff in a way that makes it easier for us to find it. The order may not make sense to a friend or parent, because we have our own personal system to categorize related or associated material.

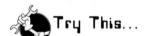

Your Turn

Put James' "secret to a good memory" into action. Choose two random facts to remember. Perhaps you can open a book and choose two sentences at random. Write each fact on a separate piece of paper. Do nothing with one fact, but with the second fact attempt to create a longer list of associations of what this fact reminds you of. Make a quick sketch of the fact if you like. Come back to these two facts in a few days to see which one is easier to remember.

Try This...

Answer these questions:

- What month is it?
- What day of the week is it?
- What year is it?

While these questions seem very easy to answer, they are more difficult than they seem, and you had to use quite a lot of memory capacity to answer them. Let's explore the memory power – all the aspects of memory – that enables you to answer these "simple" questions.

What's Going On?

Answering these questions requires a facts knowledge of the days of the week, months, and years, but it also must be updated: today's answer may not be the same as yesterday's or tomorrow's answer.

If our memory system were simple, like a date counter on a digital watch, we would be able to answer the question just as quickly on one day as on any other. However, if people in the U.S. are asked what day it is on Wednesday, it takes twice as long to answer as when they are asked on Sunday. Weekdays take longer to recall than weekend days, probably because there are five weekdays and only two weekend days. The closer the weekday is to the weekend, the faster it is recalled. The length of every day is equal, but their meaning to us is not. Why do you suppose people can identify the day of the week better for some days than others?

Your Turn

Do the same experiment over the course of the next week. Pick a few people at random and come back to them every day for a week to ask them what day it is. You'll probably need a stopwatch or a digital watch to get the most accurate results. Your answers will vary by seconds or fractions of a second. Record the times – you probably don't want to leave it all to memory! Don't let people know what you are doing. Be as inconspicuous as you can for the best results.

Try This...

Here's another activity you can do yourself or with a friend or relative as your subject. Ask each question and get a complete answer before going on to the next question. The person answering can either write the answers or say them aloud.

1) What are the months of the year? Time the answer, and don't go on to the next question until it is completely answered and you record the time it takes to respond.

2) Name the months of the year in reverse. Give your subjects time to overcome their surprise and encourage them to keep going! Write down the time it takes.

3) Name the months of the year in alphabetical order. Hang in there. You can do it. Don't forget to time the response and write down the time it takes.

What's Going On?

You or your subjects probably had no problem answering the first question, but you probably found it increasingly difficult to answer the other questions. The reason is that if you are asked to remember something in a way that is different from your usual way of remembering it, the task will be more challenging.

For the first question, you probably began by reciting the months in chronological order, beginning with January. You should have been able to list the months quickly because the months are usually organized in that order in your memory. Question two probably took longer and you may have made some errors. Question three probably took even more time. Most people make several mistakes along the way when they are remembering the months in this way.

Although you know the months and how to alphabetize, you have probably never been asked to organize the months this way, so it takes you longer to do it.

Chunking and Coding

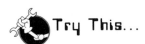Try This...

Do these four experiments alone. Then try them out on a friend or relative. Each time, you will take a quick look at letters or numbers, then you will close the book, and write down what you remember.

1. Look at these letters. Close the book. Write them down:

GEAIMNN

2. Look at these numbers. Close the book. Write them down:

4 1 2 3 6 1 0 8 3 2 4 9 7 2

3. Look at these letters. Close the book. Write them down:

MEANING

4. Look at these numbers and keep in mind the following code: begin with 4, then multiply it by 3; then multiply this product (12) by 3 again. Repeat this multiplication three more times. Ready? Close the book. Write them down:

4 1 2 3 6 1 0 8 3 2 4 9 7 2

Which task was the easiest? Which was the hardest? You looked at the same number of letters and the same number of numbers each time. So, why do you think some tasks were easier than others?

What's Going On?

You were able to remember some letters and numbers better because you chunked them. That is, you organized them into one or more meaningful units. A unit of memory is called a **chunk**. When remembering information, chunking is the process of using a code to organize the individual items into larger units or chunks of memory. In the first and third examples, the individual letters were organized into the larger unit of a word. The code used for this was the English language. When you "chunk" GEAIMNN into MEANING, it is easier to remember.

The second and fourth examples demonstrate that knowing a code increases the capacity of memory and the ability to remember. In this case the code is the math instructions. You don't have to memorize any of the numbers; the code tells you where to begin, what to do, and where to stop.

Your Turn

Read the following lists quickly and see if you can devise a code to help you remember them.

MT VW WE VH 1F BI
817 263 544 536 271 891

If you had to reproduce the two lists above, the simple way would be to notice that the top line includes four well-known acronyms. The first is MTV. Can you guess the others now? The bottom row includes the multiples of nine in descending order from 81. How would you write the two lists to make them easiest to remember?

The Importance of Context

**Try This...**

This experiment will demonstrate the importance of context. First, read this brief story just once.

> With hocked gems financing him, our hero bravely defied all scornful laughter that tried to prevent his scheme. "Your eyes deceive," he had said. "An egg, not a table, correctly typifies this unexplored planet." Now three sturdy sisters sought proof. Forging along, sometimes through calm vastness, yet more often very turbulent peaks and valleys, days became weeks as many doubters spread fearful rumors about the edge. At last from nowhere welcome winged creatures appeared, signifying momentous success.

Close the book and write down as much as you can remember of the story. When you're finished, open the book and find out what to do next.

Now read the story again, but, this time, keep this context in mind: the story is about Christopher Columbus' voyage to America.

What's Going On?

Context is background information such as the time, place, and circumstances of an event. In this story, the context includes your knowledge of Columbus's belief that the earth is round not flat, that he and his crew traveled in three boats named after females, that the voyage was difficult, that some of the sailors thought they would sail off the edge of the earth, and that all were relieved when they saw sea gulls, signaling that land was near.

Two researchers, Dooling and Lachman, found that people who had been given the context for this story remembered much more than those who had not. The main function of context is to provide an expectation before reading to which the information can easily be related. A context makes the information memorable because the information is connected in a meaningful way. A title usually announces an overall context and gives you an idea of what to expect. Knowing an author's purpose also helps you understand a text because it provides a context for understanding what the author says. Knowing the context helps us understand and remember what we read.

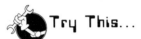**Try This...**

Let's follow the same procedure for the next two stories. Read the stories quickly including the titles, close the book, and write down what you remember.

Watching a Peace March from the 40th Floor

The view was breathtaking. From the window one could see the crowd below. Everything looked extremely small from such a distance but the colorful costumes could still be seen. Everyone seemed to be moving in one direction in an orderly fashion, and there seemed to be little children as well as adults. The landing was gentle, and luckily the atmosphere was such that no special suits had to be worn. At first there was a great deal of activity. Later, when the speeches started, the crowd quieted down. The man with the television camera took many shots of the setting and the crowds. Everyone was very friendly and seemed glad when the music started.

Don't look at the next story just yet. Close the book and write down what you remember!

A Space Trip to an Unexplored Planet

The view was breathtaking. From the window one could see the crowd below. Everything looked extremely small from such a distance but the colorful costumes could still be seen. Everyone seemed to be moving in one direction in an orderly fashion, and there seemed to be little children as well as adults. The landing was gentle, and luckily the atmosphere was such that no special suits had to be worn. At first there was a great deal of activity. Later, when the speeches started, the crowd quieted down. The man with the television camera took many shots of the setting and the crowds. Everyone was very friendly and seemed glad when the music started.

Write down what you recall. Don't look back at your recollection for the previous story.

Now compare what you wrote each time. What do you notice about your recall?

What's Going On?

As you have realized, the two stories are the same except for the title. The activity above is a demonstration of how context, when deliberately altered, can affect memory. In this case, the context — or background information — is the title of the story.

Now look more closely at what you recalled and wrote down. In your first recollection, did you write down anything about the sentence "The landing was gentle, and luckily the atmosphere was such that no special suits had to be worn"? In one experiment, only 18% of the people recalled something about the sentence from the first story.

With a different context, however, recollection of this sentence is improved. When people read the second story with the title "A Space Trip to an Unexplored Planet," the sentence "The landing was gentle..." makes sense. Of those who read the story with this title, 53% recalled the sentence.

The word "context" comes from the Latin word meaning "to weave together." When information is presented in a context that is meaningful to an individual, it is remembered more easily. Information is woven into an already meaningful background.

Your Turn

Have two friends do the same experiment. Give one of them the story with one title, and the other one the story with the other title. Then compare what they remembered about the story.

More Fun

Do the same experiment, but this time choose your own passage. Use a passage from a textbook you are using in school, a library book, or a passage from the Web. You could also choose a poem or song lyrics.

First, give your friends the passage without a title. Then give each one a different title. See how the two contexts (the titles, in this case) influence which parts they remember.

Interference with Memory

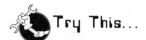

Try This...

Read the following phone numbers, close the book, and write them down from memory:

883-2299
542-5218

How did you do? OK, now try it with this pair of phone numbers. Close the book quickly. No second peeks.

524-5318
542-5218

How did you do this time? Why do you think one task was easier than the other?

What's Going On?

Sometimes we experience interference with our memory. This is especially true if we are trying to remember information that is similar, for example, trying to remember the phone numbers of two people. If the first number is 524-5318 and the second is 883-2299, you will experience less interference between the two numbers than if the second number were 542-5218.

Two general factors in interference are (1) the more similar the items, the more interference, and (2) the longer the interval between the first and second event, the less interference. Supposing your mom is making a list of your friends to invite to your birthday party. She asks you to tell her the names of your friends. It so happens you have a friend named "Sean" and one named "Shawn," so you say "Sean," but forget to say "Shawn." You have a friend named "Timmy" and one named "Tyrone," but you remember to say both names for your list. Since "Sean" and "Shawn" sound alike, your mind perhaps interfered by saying you'd already said the name once. But, the same wouldn't happen to "Timmy" and "Tyler" because there's not much similarity to these names.

69

Memory and Importance

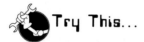

Try This...

Read the following list of words once. When you are done, quickly close the book and see how many you can write down.

eyeglasses

bottle

moon

beehive

curtain

seven

ship

wheel

the

after

What's Going On?

If you are like most people, you probably remembered more words from the beginning and the end of the list than from the middle of the list. In one study, when people were asked to memorize a list of words, they recalled a word at the beginning of the list 70% of the time, words in the middle less than 20%, and words at the end almost 100%.

We seem to notice change and points of transition very easily. Beginnings and endings of events are common transition points. If you turn on a fan, at first you are probably very aware of the noise, but over time you probably stop hearing it. Our senses respond most at the beginnings and endings of stimuli; in between, they **habituate,** or stop responding. Similarly, we tend to remember the beginning and ending of an event better than the middle, and the ending better than the beginning. From a survival standpoint, this is a very helpful adaptation. Our species evolved on the savannahs of Africa where, even today, a person needs to be alert for large predators, such as lions or leopards. Quickly noticing a change – a sudden movement, the behavior of other animals, a scent in the air – has probably saved a human life countless times. In the bustle of the large cities that many of us live in today, this same adaptation has probably saved many lives by alerting a pedestrian to an on-coming vehicle.

Having better recall of beginnings is an example of what is called the effect of **primacy.** Having better recall of endings is an example of the effect of **recency**. The principles of primacy and recency in memory have been extensively demonstrated experimentally using lists of nonsense syllables. They also hold as general principles in many areas of life, from the basic characteristics of the sensory systems to our involvement in films, sporting events, and friendships. You can probably remember clearly the day you met your best friend or the day you broke up with a boyfriend or girlfriend, but what about all the time in between?

When dramatic, life-altering, or life-threatening events happen, people are likely to recall an unusual amount of detail about their circumstances at the time the event occurs. Psychologists Brown and Kulik called these vivid memories **flashbulb memories** because it seems as though, at these tense moments, the mind "takes a picture" of the scene.

Two explanations have been offered for this phenomenon. The first is that the heightened emotions of the person at the time of the event increase the strength of the person's memory. After all, if some cue saved you from that human-eating big cat or those urban metal monsters, you'd want to make sure you didn't forget it!

The other proposed mechanism for flashbulb memories is that these memories are recalled with such detail because we use them as reference points in our lives. In our personal histories, these exciting events are turning points and we replay them over and over.

Your Turn

Conduct your own experiment to demonstrate our ability to remember endings and beginnings better. Create your own word list of ten to twenty words and see how many words your friends can recall after just one peek.

Or try to improve your memory with a current list of vocabulary words from school. Every time you sit down to study, rewrite the list with new words at the beginning and ending.

More Fun

Many people also have vivid flashbulb memories when dramatic events occur on the national scene. Many older people alive today can vividly recall what they were doing when they heard the news that President John F. Kennedy was assassinated in 1963. Others can recall what they were doing on the day the space shuttle Challenger exploded upon lift-off in 1984 or when planes crashed into the World Trade Center in 2001. Interview some friends and relatives and ask them if they remember dramatic events like this and what they were doing at the time. If they can, you'll have some examples of flashbulb memory. Compare their memories of what they were doing on the days of these dramatic events to some randomly picked dates of the same year.

Test Your Memory on Chapter 4

Choose the correct answer.

1. Which is a basic principle of memory?
    a. memories involve associations
    b. memories are simpler than actual experience
    c. we remember meaningful events
    d. all of the above

2. Memory is organized around
    a. associated events or ideas
    b. the middle of an event
    c. the least important idea
    d. context clues

3. Which mental process aids memory?
    a. chunking
    b. coding
    c. both a and b
    d. none of the above

4. Which of the following can aid memory?
    a. pre-coding
    b. contacts
    c. context
    d. clunking

5. What is the name given to vivid memories after experiencing a dramatic event?
    a. instant
    b. flashbulb
    c. photographic

Keep It In Mind

Key-Word Notes is another strategy that can help you in school. Pair up with another student. Read a section of the text and, individually, identify three or four words that you think are key – words that will help you remember important chunks of information. Write the words down. Then explain to each other what words you chose, why you chose them, and what information you think they will help you remember. Go on to the next section of the text and do the same thing. Repeat this process until you've completed your reading. At the end, put the book aside and write a summary that includes all of the key words you wrote down.

And don't forget – always pay attention to the context. When reading a textbook, don't skip the titles or the passages in italics or parenthesis.

Finally, if you are studying a list, rewrite it several times over the course of your study period so that the information in the middle has a chance to appear at the beginning or end of the list!

Answers for Chapter Four
    1. d, 2. a, 3. c, 4. c, 5. b

 **False Memory**

When people think of remembering and forgetting, they usually assume that what is remembered or forgotten is a true event. However, as you read earlier in Bartlett's studies of serial and repeated memory (page 41), our memories may morph — shifting or changing in complex ways. For example, a mother recalls telling her young daughter stories about her own childhood. Her daughter not only enjoyed the stories, sometimes she would later repeat them with one important difference: The daughter would tell the stories as if they had happened to her, not to her mother. Moreover, when challenged, the daughter insisted that they were her stories. But memories don't only morph; they can also be constructed. False memories then range from changes in true memories to actual false recollections — memories of events that never actually happened.

Memory is complex. Not only are there many different kinds of memories, there are also several different ways of understanding how memory works. We will examine each of these ways of understanding how memories are made and lost individually to help us understand memory and forgetting as a whole.

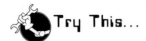

Try This...

Ask your friends to participate in an experiment, and when you have their agreement, divide them into two groups:

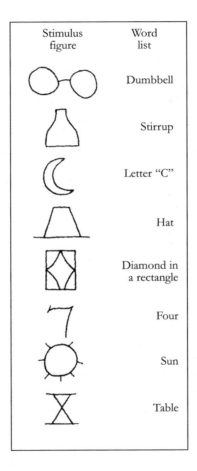

Show one group of your friends the images at left, telling them what the images depict from the word list. Tell them that you will ask them to reproduce these drawings from memory the next day.

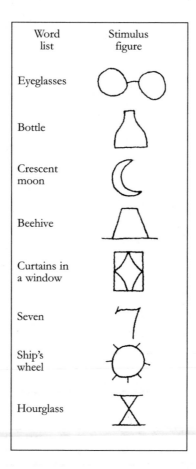

Word list	Stimulus figure
Eyeglasses	
Bottle	
Crescent moon	
Beehive	
Curtains in a window	
Seven	
Ship's wheel	
Hourglass	

Show another group of your friends these images, telling them what the images depict from the word list. Again, tell them that you will ask them to reproduce these drawings from memory the next day.

Come back to these same two groups of friends the next day and ask them to reproduce the series of images. Did you notice how the reproduced drawings of each group were affected by the word list?

What's Going On?

Memories can be affected by suggestions. In a study designed by Elizabeth Loftus people were shown a reddish-orange disc. One group was told it was a tomato; the other group was told it was an orange. Later, the two groups were shown colors and were asked to use their memories to select the color that most closely matched the color they had seen. The group that had been told the disc was an orange selected a color closer to orange; the group that had been told the disc was a tomato selected a color closer to red. Did you come up with similar results?

Loftus later found that suggestions in an interview could lead many people eventually to recall being lost in a shopping mall. This study was based on a less formal experiment. An older brother, Jim, had asked his teenaged brother, Chris, to try to remember being lost in a shopping mall when he was five. After several days, Chris "remembered" being lost in the mall quite distinctly, although he evidently had never really been lost there.

The shopping mall experiments may show the power of association as well as suggestibility.

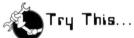 Try This...

Read the following list to a friend or relative:

**thread, pin, eye, sewing, sharp, cloth,
thimble, haystack, injection, point, hurt**

Now read them this second list and ask them to identify which words were or were not in the first list.

**thread, sewing, door, sleep, needle, cloth,
awake, thimble, hurt, candy, haystack**

Can you make a guess about which words will be identified correctly and which word is most likely to be remembered mistakenly?

What's Going On?

Psychologists Henry Roediger and Kathleen McDermott conducted a similar experiment. Most people would correctly remember "sewing" and correctly identify that "sleep," "candy," and "awake" were not heard; however, most would also falsely remember "needle." The false memory probably arose because "needle" was so clearly associated with the actual words: "thread," "pin," "thimble," or "sewing."

This study suggests that the power of suggestion in the shopping mall studies was likely aided by the familiarity of shopping malls and stories of children getting lost there and in other places.

A Dutch study suggests that these effects are not just found in laboratories. The psychologists explored memories of a major event that happened ten months earlier, in October 1992. A cargo plane had taken off from the Amsterdam airport, had engine failure, and crashed into an eleven-story apartment building, killing 44 people. TV news had covered the accident extensively. The psychologists asked members of the community, "Did you see the television film of the moment the plane hit the apartment building?" and 55% said yes, that they remembered seeing that film. However, there was no film of the actual crash. Once again, the power of suggestion (the question took it for granted that the film existed) and association (the many memories, including memories of the crash scene) probably contributed to this result.

Daniel Schacter and his colleagues have studied the way the brain works when true and false memories are recalled. Recently, researchers have been able to learn much more about the details of brain activity using new technologies, such as PET scans (positron emission tomography) and fMRI (functional magnetic resonance imaging). Images of the brain taken by PET scans or fMRI show that brain activity is not very different for false or true memories. An area of the brain associated with memory, the **hippocampus**, showed the same patterns of activity. This similarity would explain why Chris "remembered" being lost in the mall or Dutch TV viewers "remembered" seeing a crash that was not filmed.

Your Turn

Choose a memorable experience you shared with someone close to you. Try to choose an experience that you may not have talked about a lot recently. Get together with that person and, without talking about the experience, each of you write down what you remember in as much detail as you can. When you are both finished, compare your recollections of the event. What do you notice about the two recollections? How might you explain the similarities and differences?

Did You Know?

In Spring 2004, researcher Elizabeth Loftus appeared on the TV show "Scientific American Frontiers" with Alan Alda. In this episode, Loftus discusses her research into creating false memories. She demonstrates her persuasive techniques on Alda himself. She is able to get him to question whether or not he ever got sick from eating hard-boiled eggs. Alda goes from being entirely sure that he didn't to being not sure. (For more information on false memories and other memory issues discussed in this episode visit this PBS website, http://www.pbs.org/saf/1402/index.html.)

Our memory is good enough for everyday life. We do not usually need to know things in complete detail. But when details are important, perhaps a matter of life and death, false memory reveals that our memory can become a problem. In courts of law, questions of guilt and innocence often are decided by a witness who stands, points a finger at someone, and says, "It's him. I saw him do it with my own eyes."

We have such confidence in our memory that the power of eyewitness testimony is not easily overcome, even if it is successfully challenged by other testimony or methods of discovery. One recent analysis examined 40 cases of people who had been convicted of crimes, but then later cleared when DNA evidence established their innocence.

In 36 of these 40 cases, mistaken eyewitness testimony had been a critical factor in the mistaken finding that the people were guilty. Clearly, many innocent people have been accused and sentenced to prison on the basis of the testimony of an eyewitness. An understanding of false memory should make us more careful.

Test Your Memory on Chapter 5

Answer true or false.

1. Memories are much simpler than actual experience.

   a. True   b. False

2. Memory can shift in complex ways.

   a. True   b. False

3. We cannot construct memories of an event that never happened.

   a. True   b. False

4. Suggestions do not influence our memories.

   a. True   b. False

5. False memories can arise from mistaken associations.

   a. True   b. False

Keep It In Mind

Read, Talk, Write is another strategy you and a partner can use to help you remember your schoolwork. Find another person who is reading the same text. Individually, read silently for a few minutes. Then close your books and take turns talking about what you just read. While one talks, the other listens. After you have both talked, write down what you have learned so far. Repeat this process until you have completed your assignment.

Answer Key for Chapter Five
   1. a, 2. a, 3. b, 4. b, 5. a

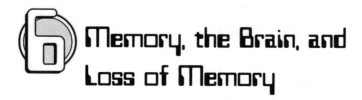

Memory, the Brain, and Loss of Memory

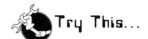 Try This...

Pretend you are a medical student and you suspect Mr. H. M., a patient, has some memory problems resulting from a head injury. Read the following interview and use the knowledge you have gained from this book to see if you can detect Mr. H. M.'s problem:

>   **You:** Good morning, Mr. H. M.
>
>   **H. M.:** Good morning.
>
>   **You:** I wonder whether you could answer a few questions?
>
>   **H. M.:** Fine, go ahead.
>
>   **You:** Who was President of the United States during World War II?
>
>   **H. M.:** Franklin Roosevelt, later Truman.
>
>   **You:** What did Truman do when a national rail strike was threatened?
>
>   **H. M.:** He nationalized the railways, or he threatened to.

The questions and answers continue, until you begin to wonder whether there is any deficit in memory. Then the phone rings, and you excuse yourself to take an urgent call. You return.

> **You**: Sorry, Mr. H. M., to interrupt our session.
>
> **H. M.**: I beg your pardon, have we met before?
> I don't seem to remember you.

Before continuing, take a moment and describe what you think is happening.

What's Going On?

Did you notice that H. M. cannot remember what just happened to him? He lives in a kind of perpetual present. Everything he has experienced since his injury is forgotten almost immediately, as when you jot down a phone number and then forget it quickly. But notice that H. M. retains his memories of language and what an interview is, and remembers quite a lot from years ago.

Different forms of damage to the brain can affect the storing and retrieval of memory. This search for how memory is distributed in the brain is one of psychology's most exciting pursuits. **Epileptic seizures** often over-stimulate and damage parts of the **limbic system** (the part of the brain which includes the **hypothalamus**, the **hippocampus**, and the **amygdala** and is concerned especially with emotion and motivation). When the hippocampus is affected, either by the epilepsy or by subsequent surgery, there are profound affects on memory. The interview with H. M. is an example of how damage to the hippocampus can affect memory.

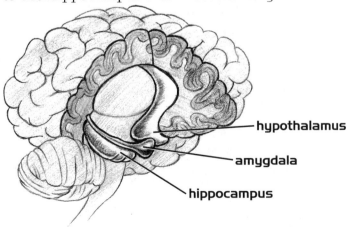

hypothalamus

amygdala

hippocampus

Amnesia is the general name for deficits in learning and memory that occur abruptly, especially following some kind of injury to the brain. Amnesia can take many different forms and can involve injuries to many different areas of the brain. People may lose the ability to recall past events or current events, in learning new distinctions or remembering old ones, or in recognizing people or places.

Some kinds of memory loss are linked to aging. As people in the U.S. live longer and as the large baby-boom generation of the 1950s enters its retirement years, age-related loss of memory (also known as **dementia**) is becoming an increasing concern. **Alzheimer's disease**, for example, is one of the major age-related forms of memory loss. People with Alzheimer's begin to have their brain cells die. A number of factors, from having certain genes to different diets, to amount of education, have been related to risk for Alzheimer's, but its causes remain uncertain.

In early stages of Alzheimer's, people experience loss of memory for recent events, disorientation in noisy or complex environments, and changes in emotions and personality. In later stages, the memory losses become increasingly severe. People may wander, be angry and confused, stop recognizing their closest family members, and lose the ability to care for themselves. Finally, patients lose the ability to communicate and walk, and eventually the disease leads to death. In the year 2000, about 4 million people in the U.S. had Alzheimer's. By 2050, it is estimated that 14 million people will suffer from this disease. Loss of memory is devastating for the person and for friends and family. Taking care of someone who has lost his or her memory is very difficult. Researchers are actively studying the causes of Alzheimer's and other related diseases and searching for effective treatments.

Did You Know?

According to the Alzheimer's Association the number of Americans with this disease has doubled since 1980 to 4.5 million. It is estimated that by 2050 this could increase to between 11.3 to 16 million people. In a 1992 Gallup poll, 10% of

Americans said they had a family member with Alzheimer's and 33% said they knew someone with the disease. The national cost for caring for these individuals is at least $100 billion. The Center for Disease Control estimates that 14% of patients in nursing homes have Alzheimer's and it is the seventh leading cause of death among Americans. For more information, go to:

(http://www.alz.org/AboutAD/statistics.asp) &

(http://www.cdc.gov/nchs/fastats/alzheimr.htm)

Test Your Memory on Chapter 6

Fill in the blanks with the correct answer.

1. Different forms of damage to the brain can affect the _____ and _____ of memories.

2. Damage to an area of the brain called the _____ can have a profound affect on memory.

3. People may lose short-term memory but still retain _____ memory, memories of language, and/or _____ memories.

4. _____ is a general name for a memory loss that occurs abruptly.

5. _____ _____ is a major age-related form of memory loss.

Keep It In Mind

Head injuries from falls can also cause damage to the brain and loss of memories. Many students resist wearing bicycle helmets or appropriate protective headgear for other activities. While we may resist wearing headgear because we don't think it is cool or we don't want to mess up our hair, helmets are important in protecting our brains in the event of an accident.

Answer Key for Chapter Six
1 .storage and retrieval, 2. hippocampus, 3. long-term, procedural, 4. Amnesia 5.Alzheimer's disease

Traumatic Memories and Healing Narratives

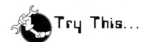

Try This...

Here's a story of one person's experience of receiving a traffic ticket. Can you sympathize with the author's reaction?

Recently I received a $300 speeding ticket while vacationing out of state! I was driving 30 mph in a 15 mph school zone. I had missed the sign and was unaware that I was in a school zone. It was 1 p.m. and there were no children on the sidewalk, there were no yellow school buses in sight, and there were no parents waiting by their cars to pick up children. In fact, the only pedestrians in sight were the two police officers jumping out from behind a bush to ticket unsuspecting drivers. By the way, this happened on August 2nd when most schools are on vacation. I complained to the officer, but he did not seem to care. I tried to remain calm expecting to receive a fine of about $75. When I saw that the fine was $300, I was outraged!

For several days I could think of nothing but this ticket. I complained to anyone who would listen including the local Visitor's Bureau and the hotel manager. Most people were kind and understanding and allowed me to "vent." My wife and son were very supportive as they endured the hundredth retelling of this story. Finally, I started to feel better and got back to enjoying my vacation. What do you think made the difference? After all, I still owed the $300!!

Have you had a recent experience that provoked anger and frustration? Write down your recollection of the experience before reading further.

What's Going On?

While the above experience hardly qualifies as a traumatic event, it was distressing enough to provoke intrusive thoughts and memories for several days. Recent psychological studies of people who have experienced truly traumatic events — wars, terrorist attacks, car accidents, fires, or domestic violence — have shown how **intrusive memories** lessen if the subject is allowed to vent.

Sometimes when people experience traumatic events, the distress caused by the event, or the **trauma**, can lead to a devastating type of flashbulb memory, with terrible memories and the emotions associated with them coming repeatedly and involuntarily. People talk of "reliving" the events over and over again. These intrusive memories may take the form of visual images, a single scene from the event or a sequence, something like a film clip being played. Sometimes the intrusive memories arise in other senses, in the form of smells, sounds, or sensations in the body.

When people continue to have such traumatic memories, they naturally experience high levels of stress, and this can lead to depression and other symptoms of serious mental disease. After the Vietnam War, many veterans came home and experienced intrusive memories for years after their return. Psychologists came to recognize this problem as a particular memory-related kind of mental disease, **post-traumatic stress disorder (PTSD)**. Although it was first diagnosed among veterans of war, PTSD can also occur after car accidents, fires, physical attacks, rapes, and other

traumatic events. People not only recall the events, but relive the stress.

Memory can help cure mental disease. Stevan Weine, a psychiatrist from Rutgers University, and colleagues worked with refugees from the terrible ethnic violence, terrorism, and wars of the former State of Yugoslavia in the 1990s. Many of the refugees suffer from PTSD. Weine found that people can reduce the intrusive memories if they tell their stories, and if they relate their individual experiences to the stories of others.

As we saw with our driver who got the speeding ticket, the value of telling your troubles seems to work even for people who do not suffer from PTSD. Psychologist James Pennebaker studied the effects of having people simply write about difficult experiences in their lives. In these studies, people don't have to share their writings with anyone; they just need to express themselves. Yet, nevertheless, they not only report better moods and better life experiences (higher grades for students, fewer doctor visits, better success at work), they also show measurably higher levels of **T-cells**, part of our immune system. In short, if repeatedly reliving painful memories can cause distress, expressing those memories as stories, as narratives, can lead to healing.

Test Your Memory on Chapter 7

Match the correct answers.

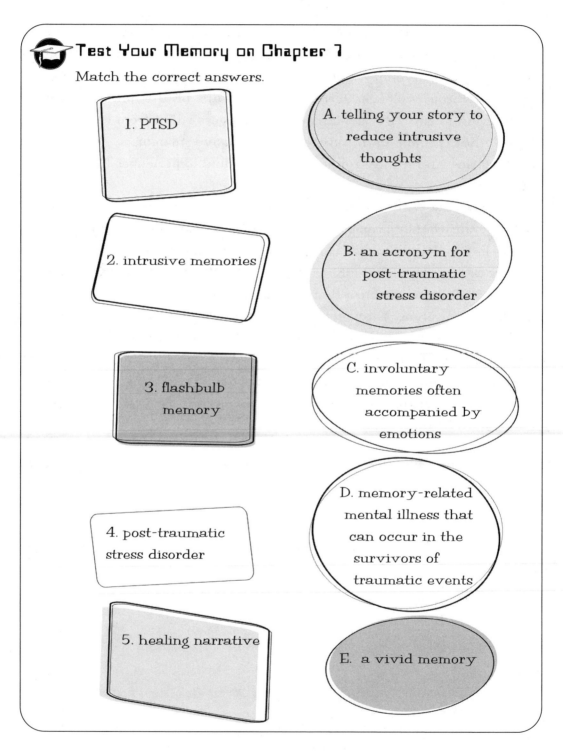

1. PTSD

A. telling your story to reduce intrusive thoughts

2. intrusive memories

B. an acronym for post-traumatic stress disorder

3. flashbulb memory

C. involuntary memories often accompanied by emotions

4. post-traumatic stress disorder

D. memory-related mental illness that can occur in the survivors of traumatic events

5. healing narrative

E. a vivid memory

Keep It In Mind

Many students face difficulties in school. Sometimes students are distracted by intrusive thoughts or memories that make it difficult to pay attention in class or while doing homework. These intrusive thoughts don't have to be just connected to a traumatic event. If you are having some problems, try talking to someone you can trust – a parent or a school counselor. If you don't want to tell your story to another person, write it down in a diary or journal.

Answer Key for Chapter Seven
   1. B, 2. C, 3. E, 4. D, 5. A

Powerful Memories

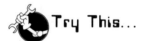

Try This...

How many times have you heard someone say, "I'll never forget the time I..."? Even though we often forget new things we learn, many important events seem almost impossible to forget. Read the following story that illustrates an extreme form of this phenomenon. When you have finished reading, refer back to the three principles of memory discussed in Chapter 4 and see how many of these principles you can identify in this story.

I'll Make You Remember

One day, Latif the Thief ambushed the commander of the Royal Guard, captured him and took him to a cave. "I am going to say something that, no matter how much you try, you will be unable to forget," he told the infuriated officer. Latif made his prisoner take off all his clothes. Then he tied him, facing backwards, on a donkey.

"You may be able to make a fool of me," screamed the soldier, "but you'll never make me think of something if I want to keep it out of my mind."

"You have not yet heard the phrase which I want you to remember," said Latif. "I am turning you loose now, for the donkey to take you back to town. And the phrase is: 'I'll catch and kill Latif the Thief, if it takes me the rest of my life!'"

(*Thinkers of the East*, Idries Shah, 1982)

Now make a list of the principles in Chapter 4 that are illustrated in this story.

What's Going On?

As William James suggested, remembering an event successfully depends on the number of associations we have to a particular event. When something arises in consciousness, all associated memories arise with it. Associations may be facts, visual, or emotional. Something is meaningful to us because it evokes many associations. Because the most meaningful information has the most associations, it is remembered better. They cluster, as James wrote, "like grapes to a stem." Each time we think about something, we increase the number of associations we have with it, and our memory for it is improved.

Generally, then, the more associations an event has, the more memorable it is. Why is Latif so sure the commander will remember the phrase? All the words in the phrase are associated in his mind with other information — both facts and experiences memories. Every time the commander looks at himself, the donkey, or anything else as he rides back to town, he will be reminded of how he got to be in this humiliating situation. And every time he thinks of that, he is likely to think again about how he will get revenge on Latif. Every image in his mind of another way of catching and killing the thief will add more and stronger associations to the phrase Latif wants him to remember. Over time, the phrase will be associated so strongly with so many of these other things that it will be impossible to forget.

Because Latif understands the nature of remembering and forgetting, he knows that the commander will go on thinking about the phrase, constructing more and stronger associations between it and other knowledge all the time.

**Try This...**

Try to solve this mathematical equation in your head:

789054.78 times 657483.86 equals?

Can you do it? Can you do it quickly?

What's Going On?

If you are like most people, you would probably feel a lot more comfortable with your answer if you could have used a calculator. As with any human ability, there are some people who excel, who develop extraordinary memories. Some people can play (and win, mostly) as many as 60 games of chess blindfolded. Some people can even multiply long numbers in their heads as fast as a calculator such as 789054.78 times 657483.86. One man could look at 70 unrelated words and recall them perfectly a day later, and sometimes even a year later. These feats are made possible by applying the principles of memory and the memory-improvement techniques described above, such as making a memory meaningful and increasing the number of associations you have for a memory.

Those famous chessmasters who can play several games at once blindfolded don't have supernatural memory but are simply able to combine or chunk larger units of a chess game than can ordinary chessplayers (see the earlier section in Chapter 4 on chunking and coding).

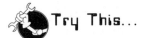**Try This...**

Look at this image:

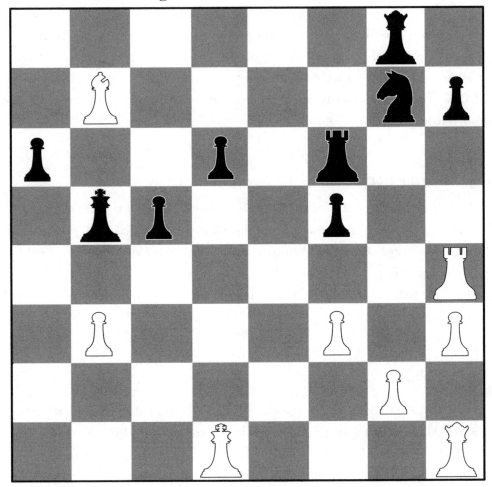

This is a fairly common arrangement of chess pieces during an actual game. Take another quick look, now close the book and try to reproduce it quickly.

What's Going On?

Unless you are an avid chess player, you probably had some difficulty getting it just right. If you have never played chess, you probably found this impossible. One study found that chessmasters are able very quickly to reproduce most common chess arrangements; beginners could not. The complex arrangement formed one simple meaningful chunk of information to the masters. However, when researchers Chase and Simon placed the chess pieces on a board at random, masters and beginners were equally poor at reproducing the positions. The random placement did not correspond to any "chunk" or meaningful pattern that the master could recall.

 ### Did You Know?

World records exist for all kinds of feats of memory — from memorizing random numbers to memorizing historical dates. Check out the website for Memory and Mental Calculation World Records (http://www.recordholders.org/en/list/memory.html) for the statistics on these and many other worldwide memory contests.

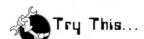 ### Try This...

Find a current list of spelling words. If you don't have a current list, make a list of ten words chosen at random. Be sure to include some unfamiliar words. Now choose a room to complete this activity. Look around the room and associate each word with a particular place in the room. Review the spots where you "placed" each word before reading on. In the next few days, come back to this room and look at each place you associated with a word. Try to recall the word — and the correct spelling — after you have looked at the spot where you "placed" it.

What's Going On?

The most famous case of memorization is "S.," who was studied by the Russian psychologist Luria. To gain a sense of the greatness of S.'s feats, study this arrangement of numbers for three minutes:

5639089728788992III389763009

Now try to reproduce it without looking at it again.

S. was able to do it in 40 seconds. Even more impressively, he could repeat it several months later! Luria writes: "The only difference in the two performances was that for the later one he needed time to revive the entire situation in which the experiment had been carried out; to 'see' the room in which he had been sitting; to 'hear' my voice; to 'reproduce' an image of himself looking at the board."

To aid his memory, S. encoded information with as many meaningful associations as possible. He was especially good at associating information with specific visual imagery, a process called **visualization**. When trying to recall a particular list, S. said, "Yes…yes, that was a series you gave to me once when you were sitting in your apartment. You were sitting at the table and I was in the rocking chair… You were wearing a gray suit and you looked at me like this."

S. also used the method of **loci** (placing an object in a familiar location) in remembering, and this sometimes led to interesting mistakes. Trying to recall a particular list of words, he imagined a "mental walk" but missed the words "pencil" and "egg":

> "I put the image of the pencil near a fence…the one down the street, you know. But what happened was that the image fused with that of the fence and I walked right on past without noticing it. The same thing happened with the word 'egg.' I had put it up against a white wall and it blended in with the background. How could I possibly spot a white egg up against a white wall?"

S. had an extraordinary ability to visualize, but, even so, his methods are merely extensions of the principles discussed in this chapter: making the associations between information meaningful by making those associations rich and complex. Thus, as James said at the beginning of the chapter, facts will "cluster and cling" in the mind.

Test Your Memory on Chapter 8

Fill in the blanks with the best answer.

1. Meaningful memories are those that have more _____.

2. Associations can be facts, _____, or _____.

3. A chessmaster can recall larger _____ of meaningful information.

4. The method of taking a "mental" walk relies on _____ to aid memory.

5. Rich and _____ associations aid memory.

Keep It In Mind

Many schools now encourage students to take **Cornell-style notes** that involve dividing a note page into two columns. One column is used for taking notes in class while the second column is used for reflecting on and reviewing your class notes in the evening. In this reflection column, students try to make connections or associations between notes they have taken and previous knowledge or questions that arise. Students can also use this column to make a quick drawing (or graph) of their notes. The more associations a student can make, the better chance they have for remembering their notes for tests.

Read, Talk, Draw is another strategy you can try that uses visual aids to improve memory. This strategy is a variation on Read, Talk, Write that was explained at the end of Chapter 5. The directions are the same, except you draw instead of write. Find another person who is reading the same text. Individually, read silently for a few minutes. Then close your books and take turns talking about what you just read. While one talks, the other listens. After you have both talked, draw or sketch what you have learned so far. Repeat this process until you have completed your assignment. When you have finished, write a short summary of what you have learned.

Answers for Chapter Eight
    1. associations, 2. visual, emotional, 3. chunks, 4. visualization, 5. complex

Improving Memory

One thing that we have definitely learned is that we can improve our memories – sometimes by a lot. In this chapter we will examine several principles that may help you remember things better. Read about each and then try them out in your daily life. There is no fixed order for trying out these principles. Most can be really helpful extending your cultural memory – in other words, they'll help you out in school!

Improving Memory by Changing Encoding

It is not useful to have learned something by heart if the information cannot be retrieved when needed. Exams test your ability to retrieve information, either by recognition or by recall. Have you ever heard someone say after an exam, "I knew the answer, but not the way the question was asked?" Concerning this problem, one psychologist writes:

> The critical thing for most of the material you learn in school is to understand it, which means encoding it in a way that makes it distinctive from unrelated material and related to all the things it ought to be related to in order for you to use it... The time you spend thinking about material you are reading and relating it to previously stored material is about the most useful thing you can do in learning any new subject matters.

Instead of simply memorizing by heart, ask "What does this mean?" Talking to a friend about what you have read is a good way to make sure you have grasped the central meaning. This is also one of the goals of the Cornell-style note-taking strategy discussed previously. When reflecting on the notes you have taken earlier in the day, you make an attempt to relate the notes to what you already know about the subject.

Rewriting your notes graphically can also help you remember the information. One way to do this is to create a "word web." Put the most important idea in a circle in the middle of the page. Put related ideas in circles around the main idea. Connect related ideas with a line. Vary the size of your circles so that the more important ideas are in larger circles. (See the section at the end of Chapter 3 on visual tools.)

Techniques for Improving Memory

One important way to deepen processing is to relate the information to you. Ask yourself, "What would have made me do that?" and other such questions, and try to recall whether or not the experience in question ever happened to you. This will increase the likelihood of recall. The reason for this increase in remembering may be that the richest set of associations in memory relates to ourselves. When information can be referred to an event in your own life, it is remembered longer. **Your own life experience is the most important context for remembering new information**. Try to relate material to your own past experience and knowledge. Many students find the study of psychology both fascinating and easy to grasp. Could it be because psychology is almost tailor-made for efficient studying, since its subject is *you*?

Improving Memory by Connecting It to Yourself

It is always easier to remember something according to a rule than by rote. It is simpler to remember the spelling rule "i before e except after c" and the few exceptions than to learn to spell every word containing "ie" or "c".

The best way to remember material that seems unrelated to you is to impose a context that will serve as an aid to memory or will change the material into something meaningful. Here is one of two methods for improving memory of meaningless events. Using **mnemonics** (the initial "m" is silent) is a straightforward, and sometimes fun, technique for aiding memory. There is nothing about the names of the months of the year that gives clues to the number of days they have. The rhyme "Thirty days have September..." is a mnemonic to help you retrieve that information when you need it. To remember which way to change your clocks for Daylight Savings Time, a useful mnemonic is "spring forward, fall back."

People often use mnemonics to remember names. To remember some-one named Scott McDonald, you might remember that his last name is the same as the fast-food restaurant. Mnemonics are often useful for remem-bering lists in a certain order. Try associating each item with a previous-ly learned, organized set of "peg words" such as in this example:

One is a bun.
Two is a shoe.
Three is a tree,
Four is a door.
Five is a hive.
Six is sticks.
Seven is heaven.
Eight is a gate.
Nine is wine.
Ten is a hen.

Now let's say you want to buy the following at the grocery store:

lettuce, soup, paper towels, tomatoes, and chicken

Try to visualize each of the things you need to buy with the above peg words. The stranger and funnier the association, the more likely you will remember it. For example, you might imagine **lettuce** on a bun, **soup** spilling out of your shoe, a tree with **paper towels** for leaves, **eggs** splat-tered all over the door, a hive full of **tomatoes**, and a **chicken** picking up sticks. A word to the wise: choose your mnemonic carefully. Betty Cone said she knew exactly how the principal of her school tried to remember her name: he always called her Betty Pine.

One variation on this use of visualization to aid recall is the method of loci, a memory trick devised by the Greeks and named after the Latin word for "places." This is the same method used by S. discussed in the last chapter. The method of loci creates new and different associations to improve recall. Select a group of places that have some relationship with one another. As an illustration, every day you awaken in your bedroom, wash up in the bathroom, have breakfast in the kitchen or dining room, and walk or drive along a certain route. Associate the items in a list in order with the different places, such as your bed, the sink, the dining room, and a tree that you pass by. For the shopping list used above, you could imagine that the sheets on your bed are lettuce, that you are eating soup out of the sink, that paper towels are on the dining room table, and so on. The method of loci is effective because human memory is associative, and "putting things in their place" increases the number of associations.

Summary

Memories give us a sense of continuity between past and present. The more associations we have to something, the more important or meaningful it is, and the better we remember it. We have many different kinds of memory: **Facts** and **experiences** forms of **declarative** memory, **procedural** memory, **short-term** and **long-term** memory, **external** memory, **social** memory, **recall** and **recognition**, and so on. We also have specific kinds of memory and forgetting associated with our senses (visual memory, memory for smells) and with different types of tasks (rote memory, memory for conversations, daily errands, faces, music). In one sense, our memory works like a computer, with a cycle of perceptions, storage, and retrieval. In another, it works more like exercise, changing us physically so that we are tuned in different ways to interact with our world.

Memory is **constructive**, as we build it with recollected bits and pieces to make sense of our lives. **Context** provides a means of organizing information, making it more memorable. The more meaningful the context, the better information will be recalled. We use **schemata** (organized mental processes) that we already possess to transform our memories of experience into familiar patterns. We tend to omit elements that don't fit with what we already know. Using a code to organize items in memory is called **chunking**. Knowing a code increases the capacity of memory. However, our memories are not infallible. They are influenced by previous knowledge and events between the remembered event and the attempt to recall it. We can have false memories in response to current suggestions or by overusing our associations.

Often, given evidence to the contrary we still find it hard to change what we "remember". When victims of a crime have identified the perpetrator they "remember" and are then shown a different image, this time of the actual criminal, they still cannot change their minds. Studies of people with damaged brains reveal information about how the brain stores memories. The **hippocampus** is important to memory, as demonstrated by the deficiencies of Mr. H. M., who could remember events that had occurred prior to his injury but could not remember post-injury events. **Amnesia** is the general name for abruptly induced deficits in learning and memory. Amnesia can result from damage to the frontal lobes, electroconvulsive shock, or from lesions (damage) to the hippocampus or **amygdala**. Amnesiacs who cannot recall past events may function normally in remembering post-injury information. **Alzheimer's** and other age-related memory loss (dementia) can be devastating, and unless we find some way of curing these diseases, they will become a much greater social problem as the U.S. population ages.

Traumatic memories of events like war, natural disaster, and violence can cause devastating stress, depression, and other symptoms of serious mental disease, but expressing and processing those memories can help to heal the **trauma**. And even just writing about our everyday troubles can make us healthier and happier.

We know that memory can be trained and improved by using our understanding of memory, by relating material we want to remember to our personal interests, by building contexts through repeated experience and reflection or by simple **mnemonics** (like the visual methods of relating items to a familiar set of places or a familiar series of objects).

Finally, we know that memory is an important part of what makes us human. It is what gives us a past, illuminates our present, and helps us orient to the future. Psychologists and other researchers are learning much about how we remember and how we forget; yet much about memory remains a mystery. Future generations will have much to learn about memory, and that which is learned promises to make our lives better in many ways.

Additional Classroom Activities

1. Give students the Inventory of Memory Experiences (IME) or some similar instrument and ask them to fill it out to find out what kinds of memories they are good at. Students could compare their findings. You could also ask students if they have noticed other kinds of things that they are particularly good or bad at remembering.

2. Writing task: Ask students to write about a time when they experienced a problem remembering something? Use the discussion of the memory cycle to analyze where in the cycle the problem arose.

3. Writing task: Ask students to write about how they study differently for a test if they know it is going to ask for recognition (like a multiple-choice or true-false test) from how they study if the test is going to ask for recall (like fill-in-the-blank or essay tests).

4. Ask students to keep a detailed inventory of things they do in class one day (or throughout the day). Then seal that inventory in an envelope and a week later, ask students to list all the things they can think of that they did in that time. Then unseal the envelope and have students compare the original inventory with the memory.

5. Have students do a serial reproduction task with a story. Have one student read the story, put it away, then write down his or her memory. Then have the second student read the first student's reproduction, put it away, and then write down his or her memory. Continue. Then have students analyze the story to identify information that was in the original story, that was deleted from the original, that was added to the original, or that was altered from the original. Ask students to make guesses about why the reproductions changed as they did. You could also do a variation where one group gets the story by reading it and the second group by hearing it. Does this make a difference?

6. Try an experiment where you ask students to look at a list of 20 non-sense words for 1 minute and then (a) try to recall them and (b) after trying to recall them, show them a list of 40 nonsense words and ask which were on the original list. Then ask students to look at 20 pictures of people's faces for 1 minute and ask them, after a bit of time has passed, to pick out which of 40 pictures they had seen. Have students try to find principles in the readings that will explain the results.

7. Have students try to make up a story like the hocked gems version of the Columbus story in Chapter 4, one that becomes easy to remember with a clue but is otherwise hard to get. Also have them make up number lists that can be deciphered with a code or a list of letters that can be read as abbreviations or reorganized in some other coded way.

8. Have students use the mnemonic peg words and/or the method of loci, both involving visualization, to memorize lists of information. Students could compete to see how many words they could memorize without error or how much they could improve from their initial attempts to memorize without mnemonics.

9. Writing task: Ask students to write a dialogue or a short skit that uses the information on memory to represent some kind of memory problem. Others could then read or view the skit and try to determine what the nature of the memory problem is.

10. Writing task: Ask students to write about a smell or some sounds (possibly music) that strongly remind them of some time in their life or some experience they had.

11. Have students explore how knowledge affects memory. Several tasks could be used. For example, you might ask students to look briefly at a chessboard with pieces set up in some conventional fashion and then try to reproduce the board on their own. You could then have students

calculate how many pieces they placed accurately and relate that to their knowledge of chess. You could also do this with things like sports standings, e.g., have students look briefly at soccer, baseball, football, basketball or cricket standings, then try to reproduce them from memory and relate performance to knowledge. It would also be useful to ask students to write down observations about how they remembered what they did.

12. Tell students ahead of time that some staged event is going to happen during the day (so that they don't get worried). Videotape the event. Have the camera set up and turn it on a bit before. The event should involve some sudden action, like someone the students don't know bursting into the room, grabbing something from your desk, saying something, and running off; or two students getting in a loud (scripted) verbal argument. When the event is over, ask students to write down what they saw and then compare the accounts, noticing any differences. If the event involved someone they didn't know, ask them to look at pictures of 5 people and pick which one they saw. You could use this activity to discuss the reliability of witnesses. (There are also lots of published studies and stories, fictional and nonfictional, that might be brought in here, too.)

13. Ask students to analyze the cultural memory systems that are involved in using a computer program or playing a computer game. If computers are not available, you might consider a board game, where there are written instructions and other objects that they can draw on as they play the game.

14. At the end of the activity, ask students to write up a scrapbook that summarizes the most important things they've learned about the ways that memory works and the ways that it doesn't work.

15. Have the class look at "Roshamon" and "Finding Nemo" and discuss what aspects of memory are covered in these films or by the characters in the stories. Discuss how well these aspects were depicted.

Glossary of Terms

absentmindedness, forgetting what one has just done or intended to do.

adaptation, being able to change behavior as a result of experiences.

Alzheimer's disease, a disease of the brain which causes loss in critical brain function, especially memory loss.

amnesia, loss of memory due to injury or disease to the brain.

amygdala, the small structures on both sides of the brain between the hypothalamus and the hippocampus. It seems to have to do with the maintenance and gratification of internal bodily needs and the storage of some memory processes, associations, events, individuals, or concepts that memory can be related with or attached to.

chunking and coding, the process of using a code to organize the individual items into units of memory.

context, the organization of information beforehand, therefore making it more memorable.

cultural memories, memories that are held in our languages, tools, art, buildings, books, and so on.

declarative memory, facts and experiences memory together which can be verbally expressed or scripted.

encoding, (as a memory aid), assigning distinctive "codes" or methods to a memory of a fact or event that will make it distinctive from other unrelated memories stored in the mind.

epileptic seizures, convulsive episodes caused by having epilepsy which is a disorder of the electrical rhythms of the central nervous system.

experiences memory, the store of individual experiences.

external memories, the same as cultural memories.

facts memories, knowledge of facts, concepts, and language (including the shape of letters and the meaning of words). Facts memory stores our knowledge of the world.

false memories, recollections that have been changed, shifted or morphed into mistaken associations.

flashbulb memories, vivid memories which seem as though the mind "takes a picture" of the scene.

hippocampus, information coming to the brain streams through the hippocampus. It is involved in learning, the recognition of novelty, and the storage of recent events into memory.

hypothalamus, is small and weighs only about 4 grams. It regulates eating, drinking, sleeping, waking, body temperature, chemical balances, heart rate, hormones and emotions.

intrusive memories, "reliving" events over and over again.

limbic system, a group of subcortical structures (such as the hypothalamus, the hippocampus, and the amygdala) of the brain that are concerned especially with emotion and motivation.

loci, mentally placing an object in a familiar location to aid in memory.

long-term memory, information that has been retained for more than a few seconds. (See also short-term memory.)

memory cycle, perception, storage, and retrieval.

metaphor, an aid to memory, usually a story or phrase that will symbolize the item one wants to remember.

mnemonics, a device or code aiding in remembering.

post-traumatic stress disorder (PTSD), intense stress caused by recalling traumatic events.

primacy, having better recall of beginnings, such as in a word list. (See also recency.)

recall, retrieving a memory.

recency, having better recall of endings, such as in a word list. (See also primacy.)

recognition, knowing that you have experienced something before.

rote memory, memory based on memorization.

schemata, a mental codification of experience that includes a particular organized way of perceiving and responding to situations or set of stimuli.

sense memories, recalling events and individuals through the senses: smell, sight, sound, and feeling.

short-term memory, information that is retained temporarily, for only a few seconds. (See also long-term memory.)

social memory, a type of external memory that involves what and who you know.

T-cells, cells produced in the body's thymus gland that contribute to the immune system, some do it by attacking infected cells and destroying them.

trauma, a disorder or behavioral state resulting from emotional stress or physical injury.

visualization, an aid to memory where one associates information with specific visual imagery.

APA National Standards for High School Psychology Curricula

IV. COGNITIVE DOMAIN - Standard Area IVB: Memory

		Hits Standard Well	Touches on Standard
CONTENT STANDARD IVB-1: Encoding, or getting information into memory			
Students are able to (performance standards):			
IVB-1.1	**Characterize the difference between surface and deep (elaborate) processing.**		
	a. Providing several examples of surface and deep processing		X
IVB-1.2	**Identify other factors that influence encoding.**		
	a. Demonstrating the role of imagery in encoding	X	
	b. Discussing the role of context and meaning on encoding (e.g., semantic encoding, surface processing, context dependent)	X	
	c. Discussing the role of rote rehearsal, imagery, and organization on memory	X	
CONTENT STANDARD IVB-2: Sensory, working or short-term, and long-term memory systems			
IVB-2.1	**Describe the operation of sensory memory**		
	b. Describing Sperling's research on iconic memory		X
IVB-2.2	**Describe the operation of short-term memory and working memory.**		
	a. Explaining the duration and capacity of short-term memory	X	
	b. Providing examples of the use of chunking to increase the capacity of short-term memory	X	
	c. Conducting a demonstration that uses short-term memory	X	
	d. Providing examples of primacy and recency effects	X	
	e. Discussing the concept of working memory as it relates to short-term memory (e.g., Baddeley)		X
	f. Examining the concept of serial position effect	X	
IVB-2.3	**Describe the operation of long-term memory.**		
	a. Charting the duration and capacity of long-term memory	X	
	b. Providing examples of different types of memory (e.g., episodic, semantic, implicit, explicit and procedural memories)	X	
	d. Distinguishing between implicit and explicit memory		X
CONTENT STANDARD IVB-3: Retrieval, or getting information out of memory			
IVB-3.1	**Analyze the importance of retrieval cues in memory.**		
	a. Identifying contextual and state-related cues (e.g., encoding specificity, state dependent memory, mood congruence)		X
	b. Examining problems related to retrieval, such as the tip-of-the-tongue phenomenon and context effects		X

(continued on next page)

		Hits Standard Well	Touches on Standard
CONTENT STANDARD IVB-3: Retrieval, or getting information out of memory *(cont'd.)*			
Students are able to (performance standards):			
IVB-3.2	**Explain the role that interference plays in retrieval.**		
	a. Providing examples of proactive and retroactive interference		X
	b. Relating the concept of interference to studying school-related material	X	
IVB-3.3	**Relate difficulties created by reconstructive memory processes.**		
	a. Discussing the role of reconstruction in claims of repressed childhood memories		X
	b. Hypothesizing about the role of reconstruction in cases of eyewitness testimony		X
CONTENT STANDARD IVB-4: Biological bases of memory			
IVB-4.1	**Identify the brain structures most important to memory.**		
	a. Relating case studies of damage to the hippocampus and its effect on memory	X	
	b. Reporting on conditions, such as Alzheimer's and stroke, that can impair memory	X	
CONTENT STANDARD IVB-5: Methods for improving memory			
IVB-5.1	**Identify factors that interfere with memory.**		
	b. Describing case studies that involve memory loss	X	
	c. Exploring the false memory/recovered memory controversy, as it relates to child abuse		X
	d. Explaining cross-racial eyewitness identification		X
IVB-5.2	**Describe strategies for improving memory based on our understanding of memory.**		
	a. Developing and describing mnemonic devices to help learn psychological concepts	X	
	b. Listing specific suggestions to enhance deep processing of information and to minimize the effect of interference	X	
	c. Describing how concepts such as massed versus distributed practice, over-learning, state and context dependence, and schemas might relate to studying		X
CONTENT STANDARD IVB-6: Memory Constructions			
IVB-6.1	**Describe the processes that lead to inaccuracies in memory.**		
	a. Describing research (e.g., Loftus) on the tendency to construct memories	X	
	b. Discussing the misinformation effect	X	
	c. Describing the implications constructed memories have on courtroom testimonies	X	

Web Source: http://www.apa.org/ed/natlstandards.html

College Board Advanced Placement
Psychology Standards

	Hits Standard Well	Touches on Standard
II. Research Methods		
The scientific nature of psychology is made clear through coverage of the methods psychologists use to ask and answer behavioral questions.		X
VI. Learning		
Students explore the basic phenomena of learning, **such as acquisition**, extinction, spontaneous recovery, generalization, discrimination and higher order conditioning.		X
VII. Cognition		
Students discover that cognition begins with sensory input and that information coding (the conversion of sensory input in some storable form), kinds of knowledge, and types of processing are concepts of cognitive psychology.	X	
Students learn that codes are created from cognitive processes that serve as the basis for our knowledge of the world, and that codes can be stored, recovered, and reconstructed.	X	
The distinction between procedural and declarative knowledge is emphasized, as are the distinctions between controlled and automatic processing and between serial and parallel processing.	X	
Students learn about reconstruction, complexity, episodic and semantic memory, forgetting, the role of context, and current models of memory processes and practical method for improving memory.	X	

Web Source: http://www.collegeboard.com/

National Board Professional Teaching Standard:
Adolescence and Young Adulthood Science Standards

These standards represent how *Me and My Memory* can aid a teacher's pursuit in helping students achieve science literacy as described by the National Department of Education.

	Hits Standard Well	Touches on Standard
Preparing the Way for Productive Student Learning		
I. Understanding Students		
Accomplished Adolescence and Young Adulthood/Science teachers know how students learn, know their students as individuals, and determine students' understanding of science as well as their individual learning backgrounds.		X
Establishing a Favorable Context for Student Learning		
IV. Engaging the Science Learner		
Accomplished Adolescence and Young Adulthood/Science teachers spark student interest in science and promote active and sustained learning, so all students achieve meaningful and demonstrated growth toward learning goals.		X
Advancing Student Learning		
VII. Fostering Science Inquiry		
Accomplished Adolescence and Young Adulthood/Science teachers engage students in active exploration to develop the mental operations and habits of mind that are essential to advancing strong content knowledge and scientific literacy.		X
VIII. Making Connection in Science		
Accomplished Adolescence and Young Adulthood/Science teachers create opportunities for students to examine the human contexts of science, including its history, reciprocal relationship with technology, ties to mathematics, and impacts on society, so that students make connections across the disciplines of science, among other subject areas, and in their lives.		X

Web Source: http://www.nbpts.org/the_standards/standards_by_cert?ID=4&x=44&y=6

Index